PRAISE FOR THE PRODUCTIVITY HABITS

"One line in *The Productivity Habits* stands out persuasively for me – this book will: "set you up for the act of doing whatever it is you want to do". While reading *The Productivity Habits*, I've experienced surprisingly regular personal 'aha' moments about why my habits may actually be a bad thing. I've realised that many things I take comfort in spending a lot of time on, may actually be 'fake work'. The list goes on. *The Productivity Habits* synthesizes productivity self-awareness."

Clayton Glen, Co-founder, ImaginativeHR

"Like most people, I am information rich and time poor.

"My business life risks being in permanent crisis, dominated by too much data from too many sources resulting in just too much to read. Yet working inside a consulting and legal business, I know that words must be measured and weighted and opinions considered and properly evaluated. The trouble is that this mountain of information is avalanching towards me and has become almost impossible to manage on a personal level.

"But I have discovered a book by a man who understands the way my mind organizes information. This book takes the way we really think and then combines this with a practical approach to building better information habits. Put simply, this book brings together a magic combination of mental, organizational and practical techniques and tools.

"It has helped me to find the most important snowflakes in the avalanche while measuring the exact height of the mountain."

Jim Odell, Partner, Kemp Little Consulting

TO MT AND P

THE
PRODUCTIVITY
HABITS

A SIMPLE APPROACH
TO BECOME MORE PRODUCTIVE

BEN ELIJAH

LONDON   MONTERREY
MADRID   SHANGHAI
MEXICO CITY   BOGOTA
NEW YORK   BUENOS AIRES
BARCELONA   SAN FRANCISCO

Published by
LID Publishing Ltd
Garden Studios
71-75 Shelton Street
Covent Garden
London WC2H 9JQ
info@lidpublishing.com
www.lidpublishing.com

A member of:

BPR
Business Publishers Roundtable

www.businesspublishersroundtable.com

Printed in the Czech Republic by Finidr

ISBN: 978-1-907794-83-4

Cover and page design: Laura Hawkins

CONTENTS

ACKNOWLEDGMENTS   viii
INTRODUCTION   ix

HABIT 1: CAPTURE
Ideas can strike at any time   2
Capture everything   3
Use a single bucket   5
Routing Information   6
How to write stuff down   10
The freedom to make a mess   11
A lifeboat of words   12
Your brain in your pocket   13
Key points   15

HABIT 2: PROCESSING
The Daily Review   18
The craving for completion   19
Decision tree   21
Ticked-off   24
Key points   25

HABIT 3: PROCESSING THE RIGHT TOOLS
You need to capture information   28
You need to compose information   29
Different tools have different strengths   31
Match the right tool to the job   36
Two-step working   39
Writing up   40
A heightened awareness of the way you create information   41

Better quality of ideas   42
A constraint   43
Something to cross out   44
Key points   45

HABIT 4: SITUATION
That which enables and constrains   48
Are contexts relevant?   49
The Context Triangle   51
What to look for   53
In a new situation   55
Construct a taxonomy of contexts   57
Defer tasks   61
Makes a task doable   63
Make sense of priority   64
Schedule planning   65
A sense of progress   65
Key points   67

HABIT 5: WORKING MEMORY
Writing out tasks   70
Projects affect people in different ways   71
Measure working memory   72
Using grammar to establish your ideal size of task   74
Defer the tasks   76
The optimal size of task   77
Better quality of thinking   79
Planning everything in advance?   80
Key points   82

HABIT 6: PLANNING
Projects and commitments   84
Uncovering things you care about   86

Map yourself   88
Growing branches   89
Cascade planning   92
The first step   92
Relevance and urgency   93
Working on stuff you care about   95
A sense of control   96
Key points   98

HABIT 7: ARCHIVING
Captured information that needn't be acted on or deferred   100
Retrieval of archived information   102
Build an info dump   103
Dumping stuff   106
Retrieval of information   107
A rich source of supporting information   109
Key points   111

HABIT 8: REVIEW AND COMPLETION
Shifting focus   114
Reviews   115
Situations and reviews   118
Do   121
Capture   122
Maintenance   123
Working in circles   126
A better way to handle channels   128
Key points   129

CONCLUSION   **130**
FINAL THOUGHTS   **135**
CONSOLIDATING THE HABITS   **136**
ABOUT THE AUTHOR   **138**

ACKNOWLEDGMENTS

My deep thanks to the many people who have caused me to think about their productivity, and my own. Without you, this book would have had no reason to be. Also to the team at LID, especially Laura, who took my incoherent explosions of ink and turned them into the fabulous diagrams herein, and David, who not only kept me thinking about you – the reader – but managed to convince me that the Oxford spelling system is the path of truth and righteousness.

And my profound love to my A-list, without whose relentless encouragement this book would have remained lodged in my head.

INTRODUCTION

I've spent the past few years studying, talking and writing about productivity – being productive - because I'm extremely bad at it. It's been a problem since my late teens, which is to say since I've been expected to do real work. My natural tendency is to procrastinate and to delay. I used to fall apart when I worked on anything which involved conflicting priorities and parallel demands on my attention. And the less said about my time-management skills, the better. I was a mess. Compounding it all was a long period of mental illness which made it very difficult to react appropriately to the world around me.

Left without the support systems I've built, I'm probably a lot less productive than you'll ever be.

So why should you listen to me?

I've always found that the people with the most interesting perspectives on a problem are from those who suffer from it the most. I've tried to become more productive and I think I've succeeded. I'd like to show you how. My issues were more extreme than most, but I think my problem plagues other people too. The fact that you picked up this book suggests you may be among them. I would like to give people the knowledge and the tools they need to create a better relationship with information, and improve their lives.

WHAT TO EXPECT

I wrote this book to combine the most useful ideas available about productivity with a few of my own, into a series of simple, digestible habits which are easy and rewarding to apply.

I like to think systemically about problems such as productivity; how it relates to the way people interact with information and the world around them. Even how it affects the way people think. So, this book won't be a set of loosely related tricks and simple hacks. Rather, it will describe something more akin to a consistent system. I've found there's a lot to the problem and a lot of thought that has to go into the solution. You should find that not only will it help you to become more productive, it will give you a new understanding of the way you work with information.

THE PROBLEM

"People talk often about information overload. That's not the issue. If it was you'd walk into a library and die."
                                          - DAVID ALLEN, PRODUCTIVITY AUTHOR AND COACH

Like David Allen, I don't buy the argument that information overload is the problem. Sure, the human race is dealing with an onslaught of information greater than at any point in our history. But you could have made that argument **at any point in our history**! Since the invention of the printing press and the electric telegraph, and probably since the invention of writing, the quantity of information flowing between individuals and groups has been growing exponentially. And people who work with information have been making the same complaints about it for centuries:

"There is no want of knowledge..."
"...our calculations have outrun conception; we have eaten more than we can digest."
                                          - PERCY BYSSHE SHELLEY, *A DEFENCE OF POETRY,* 1821

I think that so-called information overload is more a blockage caused by poor decisions - or lack of decisions - taken about information.

I don't know whether this is because the education system in the Western world fails to teach us about these decisions, or whether the brain is naturally untrustworthy when it comes to dealing with information. Either way, when those decisions aren't appropriate, difficulties occur. I've seen three common scenarios:

- Victims to whom "things happen" in life, who feel they do not have any control over how they deal with these things or ability to decide how they spend their time.
- Fiddlers who have a lot of control over things, but do tasks that are not going to have any meaning. Ever spent a day making tiny changes to the layout of your furniture or to your filing system? You'll know what I mean.
- Dreamers with a rich imagination regarding the kind of value they could achieve with their time, but who are unable to make it a reality. Instead, they flit from project to project with no focus or execution. This used to be my problem.

Productivity is not about how much stuff you're able to produce, how smart you're able to work, or your ability to juggle lots of spinning plates. Nor is it your ability to succeed at a job that you hate. Rather, it's a matter of mastery and perspective. Mastery over yourself and your resources, and perspective to decide what's truly important and what deserves your attention.

I often hear that striving for productivity is like fighting a losing battle. Or that my clients and colleagues have become so used to stress, fatigue and a feeling of always chasing a schedule, that the idea that things can change is almost inconceivable. Worse, some wear their crazy inboxes, manic schedules and high blood pressure as a badge of honour. It's like they're saying "I'm out of control; I'm working too hard... but I'm needed." I'd like to show you that productivity is a solvable problem; solvable by a change of thinking and habit. You'll know the difference when you begin to feel more effective. Effectiveness is more important than efficiency. When you become effective you will naturally become more efficient as you work on, and master, stuff that you care about. Three changes are needed to bring this about:

- Finding a better way of dealing with information; respecting the brain's talents and limitations so that you're not bogged down with tonnes of "stuff".
- Developing a framework to help you make decisions about what deserves your attention.
- Giving yourself the freedom to let go of both of these things in order to be creative, but with a clear way of regaining control and perspective.

When these changes become habits, you will gain both mastery and perspective. You will begin to respond appropriately to the situations in which you find yourself, and to the information which is thrown at you.

HOW TO READ THIS BOOK

Most productivity books are optimized for instruction; designed to be read from cover-to-cover as you digest the arguments in the book, or to be referenced; where you dip in and out when you need a specific reminder. Well-written instructional books often don't work as reference books because a particular concept might depend upon also reading an earlier section of the book. Before too long you need to re-read the whole thing! And vice versa, reference guides are often better at reminding than teaching.

Both these functions are important in any volume about productivity. It's important to learn the principles to apply them, but also to refer back so that you can master them. I've tried to solve this problem by structuring the book around eight habits which bring everything together into a system. The individual habits are designed to be adopted no more than one or two at a time. This will ease you gently into turning the habits into daily practice.

Each of the habit sections is structured around the habit loop; the three components of any habits which you have, or might want to adopt. In "Triggers" I'll describe the problem and show you the conditions and circumstances which will initiate the habit. You'll then be in a strong position to apply the new routines discussed in "What to do". The final part of the loop, "What you get", explains the benefits of being conscious of habits, conscious both the ways in which the trigger is satisfied and the way the habit forms a basis for a subsequent habit. Each habit, once internalized, becomes a firm foundation for the next habit.

Try to avoid taking on too much at once - it takes time to change old habits and adopt new ones. I'm using habits as a device for two reasons. First, it offers a way to turn a bunch of interesting and complex concepts into digestible chunks which are easy to adopt. Second, habits are automatic by definition. I hope that the core concepts of productivity, executed as habits, will become automatic as well; triggered with far less conscious thought that you might have imagined.

FORMING AND CHANGING HABITS

"We are what we repeatedly do. Excellence, then, is not an act, but a habit."
                                                                    - ARISTOTLE

When I was starting out trying to improve my productivity I read all the books I could find about becoming more effective, but made the mistake of assuming that because they seemed logical - and I understood them - I could click my fingers and turn them into a lifestyle. This didn't work. I'd play with a method, download the software *du jour*, and sometimes I'd even have a little success but I'd be taking on too much, too fast. Perhaps that's been your experience too. I realized that the concepts needed to be delivered in the form of habits which were easy to adopt one at a time.

At the end of his book, *The Power of Habit*, Charles Duhigg writes about how he was able to use the habit loop - a cue, routine and reward - to analyze the cravings that drove his own bad habits. This is a condensed outline of that process:

- Identify the routine you want to change
- Experiment with rewards
- Isolate the cue that triggers the routine
- Plan the change, setting alarms and triggers to pre-empt the bad routine

The focus of this book is on building habits as much as changing them. For each of the habits in this book, I offer a discussion about possible cues, an analysis of how cravings, rather than leading you astray can work to your advantage, and rewards on which you could focus, that you'll enjoy after adopting the habit. If you come unstuck, try following this outline for the building of new habits:

- What is the behaviour you want to introduce?
- What will it give you?
- How often should you perform it?
- In what context?
- Which cues could trigger the routine?
- What are your cravings in that cue? For example dristraction, progress, oprder, completion.
- What reward will the routine give you that'll satisfy the craving?

CAPTURE

TRIGGERS

IDEAS CAN STRIKE AT ANY TIME

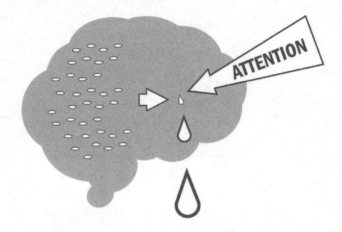

Ideas are a synthesis of both new information and information which exists in memory. They can strike at any time, and not always when convenient. You might be in a meeting that sparks off an idea which is relevant but, equally, you might find that the red cufflinks worn by the guy sitting opposite you remind you to buy new curtains for your child's bedroom.

Ideas can be useful right now, or only tangentially-related to what you're doing. This means they can be distracting, but still important.

There are lots of situations which are conducive to the formation of more and better ideas. For example, when playing, chatting with clever friends, or when you are relaxed, your mind is probably less "clenched" which lends itself to the formation of ideas. But ideas are always bubbling away in the subconscious, ready to burst into your conscious mind and come to your attention. If you accept that you don't have complete control of this process then you need to develop a good habit to help you deal with the new information you create.

CAPTURE EVERYTHING

I often have a tendency to overanalyze my ideas when they come to me. A great idea can disturb me and I'll work it through in my mind, letting it distract me. Perhaps it's the same for you. This presents two big problems:

- It's not the right time or place to work through an idea
- It can get lost in memory

It's curious that the environments which give birth to ideas are often hostile to them, and they are either lost forever or, at best, you have to try to have the idea again.

The solution is to get whatever is in your mind off your mind, and fast. It's important to get into the habit of recording anything meaningful in your mind and turning it into words. It might sound basic but it's a habit that's impeded by quite exquisite friction. Let's analyze that.

Having one idea is really a chain with three distinct parts:

1. Having the idea
2. Getting it out
3. Making a decision about it

It's like a raindrop forming in a cloud, then falling into your hand. It's hard to hold too many drops in your hand at once; some are likely to spill out onto the ground.

Some people can handle more of these chains than others. Still, when you're distracted it's easy to lose your train of thought and forget the information you're working with. You may experience this as forgetting a thought you had a minute ago. Losing a great idea in memory is immensely frustrating. Compounding this is the fact that an idea might be new, thought out for the first time, and exist only in your mind. This makes it particularly sensitive. I've even forgotten ideas while in the process of deciding what to do about them. It's maddening! When this information accumulates, it creates a colossal mess which makes it harder to engage with what you're meant to be doing.

It makes sense to turn the three parts of the chain into separate steps. What's needed is a quick method for moving information to a safe place where it can be reviewed. It's safe because its existence no longer relies on the frailties of human memory.

Then, you should be able to make quick decisions about what the information is and where it belongs. Let's look at that process in a little more detail.

WHAT TO DO

USE A SINGLE BUCKET

Capture all information, from ideas and "to-dos" to notes and shopping list items - the stuff forgotten about so easily - into a single location. Whichever location you choose - a notebook, a phone, the back of your hand - is your capture tool.

Don't worry about quality control. It's a big impediment to writing stuff down. Instead, become comfortable with the idea of recording the rubbish ideas as well as the great ideas. It's not your job, when having an idea, to decide whether it's any good or not. If it's caught your attention then it's good enough to write down. This will help the process become automatic.

When it does, the capture tool will create trust in the fact that ideas are safe. This is important because it will give you the confidence to let go of the stuff floating around in your mind so that you can focus on what you're supposed to be doing.

I'll explore tool choice in more detail later, but because you'll use the capture tool dozens of times every day, it makes sense to give it a little thought now. It will be on your person most of the time and this intimacy means you should be comfortable using it. There isn't a definitive right way to do this, but since capturing ideas is an information-dense and time-critical situation you might find that a paper notebook or voice recorder works well. The ubiquity of your smart phone means that a note-taking app could be useful too. It's important to experiment and find a tool you're comfortable using often, but once you've decided on a tool, try to stick with it.

ROUTING INFORMATION

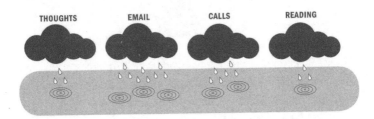

THOUGHTS   EMAIL   CALLS   READING

Ideas and spoken instructions are relatively easy to capture. But tasks often arrive as cargo, delivered by many different kinds of communication. Sometimes, these communications contain explicit instructions, for example: "Buy tea for the office". You can move this directly into your capture tool. But sometimes, information implies the task. A client might email you to confirm a meeting. This doesn't explicitly tell you to find a venue and prepare and agenda, but these are the appropriate tasks. The communication might have stimulated the idea, but most of the information has come from you.

In order to extract these tasks and place them in the capture system, the messages need to be reviewed. But different forms of communications behave differently. What's the best way to deal with them? What's needed is a system for governing the frequency with which each channel is reviewed.

I like to treat these forms of communication as discrete channels. They all have their own unique ratio of signal and noise, and they differ in their volume of traffic. You should treat a quiet letterbox differently to an exploding email inbox. Signal, or importance, is the proportion of the messages coming through the channel that deserve attention. Volume is the rate at which those messages appear.

I like to categorize channels using this principle.

- Check high volume, low importance channels less often.
- Allow low volume, high importance channels to disturb you with notifications.
- Ignore low volume, low importance channels altogether.

This is a principle which will be explored later on but, for now, try adjusting the way in which you review your channels of communication according to this principle:

- Quiet email inboxes can be checked two to four times a day.
- Re-evaluate social media; consider reducing the number of uninteresting people you follow, and check less frequently.

For a lot of people, email is a train-wreck. But the problem is human, not technological.

There are three parts to the problem:

Email is given more credibility than it deserves.
Earlier, in "Routing Information" I introduced the concepts of

"importance" and "volume" as tools for judging how often to check a channel. However, I left out the possibility that a channel could be both high importance and high urgency.

When this occurs, it means the channel is difficult to manage. This often happens with email. Email has become one of the main ways in which business is done which means that important information has become mixed with sundries and conversations. It would be nice to check it less often, but what if it contains a grenade? It's hard to deal with a channel like that.

- Consider using your mail client to separate out messages from VIPs, and filtering tools to cut out most of the rubbish you receive.
- Encourage your relatives, friends, colleagues and clients to send urgent messages via text message or phone call if they need a fast response.

These ideas won't solve the problem of email. You might develop a fantastically healthy practice of inbox hygiene but the rest of the world won't. However, this method will let you make more intelligent decisions about whether a particular channel of information is allowed to bother you. It might be a losing battle to train your friends, clients and colleagues to choose a channel based on the importance of the message, but it's definitely a battle worth fighting.

Email is fake work

The second problem with email is also the biggest problem: it's rather attractive. To monitor an inbox for incoming grenades feels like work… kind of. It doesn't present a challenge or require too much thought, but it generates a positive and rewarding feeling, as if you've done something productive even if it's sending back a pointless reply. It's the productivity equivalent of a child's favourite blanket: soothing, but it doesn't solve any problems.

If you've ever been inclined to check email compulsively, out of all proportion to its value, then you can probably sympathize.

Ambiguity in the inbox

I've found that inboxes often contain messages which have been looked at, and some that are unread. In many cases this forms a kind of rudimentary task list. However the effect is to create a massive source of ambiguity. You don't know, at a glance, whether something has been looked at, dealt with, or is about to blow up in your face.

David Allen, author of *Getting Things Done*, suggests a really useful way of dealing with this: the two-minute rule. If a particular task will take less than two minutes to do, do it right now. It'll take you about that length of time to do anything else with it so there's no point doubling up the work. It allows you to take a block of time and work top-down through your emails, deleting or archiving emails that don't matter, responding to messages which only need a quick response, and extracting tasks from those which might take a little longer.

But what if you have hundreds or thousands of unread emails, going back weeks, months, even years? Chances are, emails that old have already gone stale. It makes sense to go over all emails older than a month or so and archive them so that they're out of your inbox. Someone will have chased up anything truly important. To anything newer than that, but older than a few days, you could respond by asking the sender of important-looking messages if they still need a reply. If they get back to you, it's a new message to deal with and a fresh start.

HOW TO WRITE STUFF DOWN

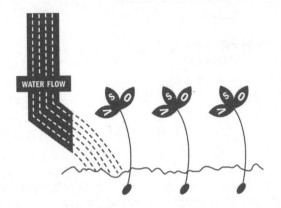

Verbs, subjects and objects form the basis of a proper sentence; a discrete unit of thought.

When writing out an idea it's easy to record it as a noun which is, for the moment, associated with the idea. For example, you might write "chocolate" when you need to buy chocolates for Mother's Day; or "£50" when they need to withdraw some cash from a cashpoint.

These nouns contain intentions. The intention is probably clear when writing the noun but it is easily forgotten. It makes sense to state them explicitly.

You write down intentions so that you can refer to them in the future, and there is a sense in which your future self is another person; just as smart as you, but someone who doesn't quite remember everything you do. Have this person in mind when writing out your tasks. You wouldn't delegate a task to someone else using a mere noun; more information is required to make sense of the task.

"Buy chocolates from supermarket for Mother's day";

Verb: Buy
Subject: Chocolates from supermarket
Object: Mother's Day

Adding a verb to the intention turns it into a task, and the object expresses the intended outcome. This sentence is a little nugget of information, supplying the intention but also the support information you need to instantly make sense it later. This makes the task much easier to do.

WHAT YOU GAIN

THE FREEDOM TO MAKE A MESS

Mess is a good thing. It is a sign that something has happened. Having the freedom to make a mess encourages you to experiment, and play. What is true of kids with their toys (and artists with their paint) is true of anyone who works with information. In fact, mess is useful. It's when you have the freedom to play, experiment, and to explore that you can be at your most productive. To make a mess requires a clear space. This space can be physical, temporal and mental. A clear workbench will lend itself to better carpentry, a clearly-defined block of time can be filled with productive work, and a clear mind will yield better ideas.

The problem is that it's hard to make a mess when you're already in one.

I used to find myself holding back thinking interesting thoughts because I'd fear forgetting them. It was absurd because it wasn't as if I could store thoughts, as yet unformed, in some stasis tank in my head to be activated and poured out at a later convenience. The mind doesn't work like that. Or I'd have the idea and focus so hard on keeping it active in my mind that I'd be unable to have another thought until I could get it out. Meantime, it distracted me from what I should have been doing. Perhaps this is familiar to you. Getting information out of your head creates a clear space in your mind where you're free to have interesting thoughts.

This habit - when it truly becomes a habit - has the power to give you a profound feeling of freedom and the knowledge that you can use your mind at any time to make a mess.

A LIFEBOAT OF WORDS

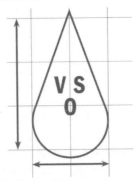

By depositing your ideas in the form of words into some tool you have made them safe against the possibility of forgetting them. This "life boat" of words has two interesting effects.

First, by taking a little time to write out the idea with a sensible amount of supporting information you can be confident that it has been properly prepared for your attention in the future. The verb and object, in particular, allow you to make sense of the task without trying to remember too much. By delegating a task to yourself in this way you have licence to let go of it - a very rewarding feeling.

Second, when you need to decide about what to do in the future, these tasks become a reliable source of information. Left to its own devices the brain only stores a fraction of the information it generates for the reference of future thought, such as planning or creativity. Recording more information like this adds the past brain's output to the present brain's input. This magnifies your quality of thought.

Ever felt a feeling of elation when reading back a great idea you had once had, but later forgot? You could have this feeling far more often.

YOUR BRAIN IN YOUR POCKET

It's not surprising to me that human memory is so bad at coping with this information sodden-world. Having said that, it's a funny thought that the human species didn't evolve to use the systems which it had itself created. We've built an environment which is completely alien to the brain and so perhaps it's inevitable that brains do such a bad job of remembering important little details. This is immensely frustrating.

Ever had that horrible "tip-of-the-tongue" feeling when you're trying to recall knowledge which you know you have, but it just won't come out? If you're lucky you'll recall the information at some later point. If not, it's probably gone forever. You might have a desperately brilliant idea in your car, but forgot it by the time you've parked, and then spend the rest of the day castigating yourself for being unable to recall it.

It feels good to know that the risk of this problem is reduced by quickly externalizing the information.

Capturing information lets you keep your conscious output safe. Consequently, you greatly reduce the risk of forgetting those details which will help you to let go and begin to trust the brain in your pockets. This will avoid you having to rethink or reinvent something which has already been accomplished.

Consider the value of this information - a collection of the connections your brain has made. The tool used to store this information is incredibly precious and may just become the most useful tool you own. The cultivation of this object is a wonderful feeling with which you can replace the annoyance of forgetting.

KEY POINTS

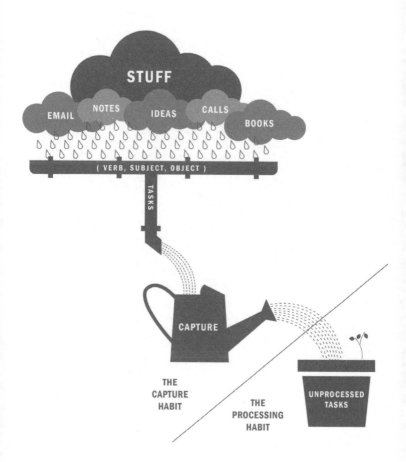

PROCESSING

TRIGGERS

THE DAILY REVIEW

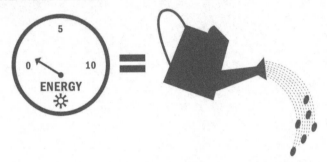

Hopefully you've become comfortable with the idea of capturing information. Now you need to do something with it. It's important to get into a habit of reviewing the list of tasks. Consistency is critical because it will prevent a build up of "stuff" from becoming a blockage. It will also help you to develop trust in the fact that your information is not lost.

Ideally, take a look at your capture tool every day. These are some good examples of the conditions which can cue this behaviour:

• When feeling tired or "brain-dead"
• As soon as you sit at the computer in the morning/evening
• Settling down for a coffee
• As soon as you get back from a meeting

These are all environments which can trigger "brain-dead", or fake work. For most people this can involve compulsively checking emails or social media, playing a quick game or fiddling with make-up. This work needs very little thought. These activities are attractive because our higher cognitive functions are inherently lazy. Because of this it's easy to waste time and procrastinate with fake work when there is something more important, if more demanding, to do.

This phenomenon - that "brain dead" tasks are easy and attractive - tells us something important. More often than not, I don't want to feel like I'm working. So instead of feeling guilty about procrastinating, perhaps it's better to use this time to perform tasks which are similarly easy but more useful.

I will show you how to review captured tasks, and make quick decisions about them. It's quick, easy to perform and can become reflexive. This makes it an ideal routine to help you replace wasteful fake work with a simple and productive habit.

An easy trigger
It's here that you will see the benefits of using a single capture tool for tasks. This "inbox", being a place where lots of sources converge, has none of the ambiguity associated with the collection of various notebooks, sticky notes plastered everywhere and forgotten reminders in your phone. This makes it easy to review the capture tool on an impulse, knowing that you're looking at everything you've captured since your last daily review.

THE CRAVING FOR COMPLETION

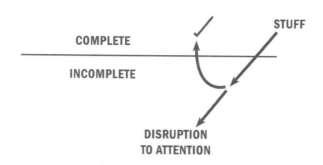

The Zeigarnik Effect: a tendency to remember patterns and objectives that are incomplete, causing intrusive and disruptive thoughts until we return to finish the task.

I often feel as if my mind is working against me; doing things that ought to be useful but are really a hindrance. The Zeigarnik effect is behind the way you try to complete songs you've heard in parts, causing the song to come to mind at inopportune moments. It causes you to remember things which are incomplete. In effect, the unconscious mind is nagging the conscious mind to define, plan and complete things which are important. These disruptive thoughts contribute to a feeling of conflict between what you're doing right now and what you feel you should be doing. The result is you are less effective at both. This urge to complete what has been started should be something you can use to your advantage. I want to show you how.

WHAT TO DO

DECISION TREE

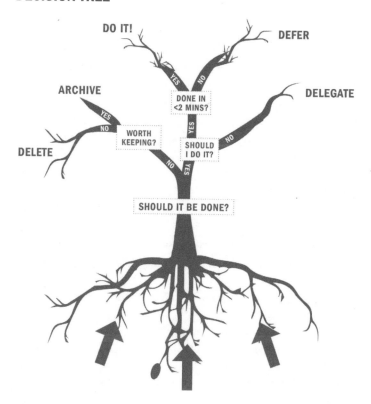

It is best to apply a set of simple verbs when processing your captured tasks. These verbs can apply to any task:

- Delete
- Archive
- Do

- Delegate
- Defer

This list forms a chain of simple decisions:

DO YOU WANT TO DO THE TASK?

This is the most important question because it allows you to apply the sort of quality control you specifically avoided when capturing the idea.

- If yes, move to the next decision.
- If no, delete or archive the task as needed; to archive the task, you could create a "someday/maybe" list or even write it up in a journal.

DELETING TASKS

- Saying "no" at this point provides focus and reduces ambiguity in the system.
- Deleting the rubbish in a single step is efficient. There will be rubbish because you've captured everything. This step restores sanity to the system.
- Everything else left in the system is something which deserves to exist.
- This begs the question: "Why does it deserve to exist?"
- The answer makes the rest of the decision making process easy.

CAN I DO IT RIGHT NOW IN LESS THAN TWO MINUTES?

The "two minute rule" is useful here for the same reason: it prevents busywork.

- If yes, do it right now. It'd take you a similar length of time to do anything else with it, so you may as well get it out of the way.
- If no, write out the task according to its intended outcome and move to the next decision.

AM I THE RIGHT PERSON TO DO IT?

Depending on what you do, this might be more or less relevant. For people working in a team it's crucial, and might even come before the two minute rule.

- If no, delegate it to the right person.
- If yes, move on to the next section.

You've filtered the list of tasks down to those which you want to do. These can't be immediately ticked off, and they can't be delegated.

This means that the only thing you can do with them is project them into the future so you can deal with them later. This is an incredibly powerful routine because it will give you a mechanism for recalling information when it becomes relevant. Later on, I'll show you how to build a sophisticated system of projects and contexts on the foundation of this habit but, for now, it's best to keep your task system simple.

There are a few approaches to this:

- Use a simple list of "to-dos", broken down into high importance/ low importance.
- A daily planner, incorporating the high/low importance idea, but on a per-day basis.
- A calendar/forecast system with no concept of importance, but that allows you to build a daily "to-do" list each day based on the calendar.

Stephen Covey, author of *The Seven Habits of Highly Effective People* described a principle of defining "big rocks"; important and proactive tasks which will move projects along. Defining a small number of these tasks every day will let you choose one as your priority. This leaves room for lots of little rocks; smaller tasks you can tick off throughout your day.

WHAT YOU GAIN

TICKED-OFF

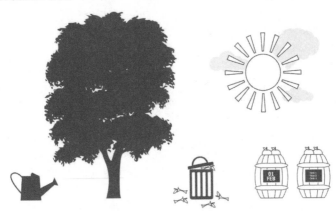

The decisions you take when processing tasks help to eliminate the ambiguities which trigger cognitive dissonance. In particular, it will give you a sense of completion. You can trust that you've made an appropriate decision about every task, and reduced the problem of conflicting priorities. The "to-do" lists means you'll recall deferred tasks at the right time, which gives you the freedom to forget about tasks you've processed. This system of projecting deferred tasks gives you more control over when you decide to work, allowing you to be proactive about the most important things to work on. Beyond this, the process of cutting out the rubbish you've captured, and ticking off the immediate actions feels good. These ticks offer a sense of progression which makes the habit, though it requires some discipline at first, "sticky" and easy to maintain.

KEY POINTS

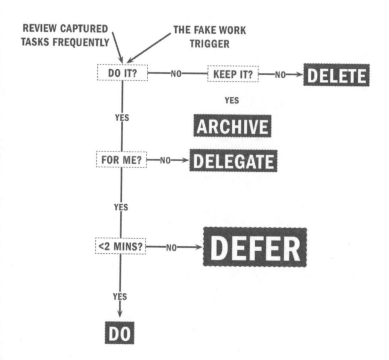

THE RIGHT
TOOLS

TRIGGERS

YOU NEED TO CAPTURE INFORMATION

The open mode of creativity is great for solving a particular problem or issue. You could even use day-dreaming as a problem-solving tool.

By now, you've established the habit of moving ideas out of your head into a capture tool. It's important to consider how you choose that tool because you're going to use it so often, and in critical situations.

The capture habit is as likely to be triggered when you're in a meeting or on a call as it is when you're going for a walk or having a coffee. The tool needs to be with you at all times. In these situations it's perfectly acceptable to capture rubbish alongside the good stuff, as long as all the good stuff is being captured. You shouldn't care about perfection. Speed and accessibility are more important.

Sitting down to write out ideas for a business, a website or a script is really just capturing your stimulated ideas. This requires a particular form of creativity called the "open mode". What does this mean?

- The mode does not usually feel focused or purposeful.
- Capturing and creating information can sometimes be playful and relaxing.
- The open mode is useful for making connections between pieces of information.
- It can often be found in situations that are social or humorous; a friendly conversation perhaps, or situations that are rich in language.

The capture tool you use when in the open mode should be quick to use, but it could also have a part to play in stimulating the creation of information.

This presents us with a contradiction. The best capture tool to carry around every day could be a smartphone but I'm better at taking notes using a pen and paper. I think it's perfectly acceptable to use the pen and paper as a kind of "ante-chamber"; quickly taking notes and drafting ideas. These can then be written up into the task system.

YOU NEED TO COMPOSE INFORMATION

You'll also find yourselves in situations where you don't need to capture or create information, but write it up, compose it, and turn it into a finished product. This might seem like a pedantic distinction from creating information but, in fact, the behaviours are quite different. Just like with processing, when writing up notes, compiling research or arranging thoughts for an email you're making decisions about what to include, where it belongs, and how best to express it.

It's the difference between writing and editing. It requires a different mode of creativity called the "closed mode".

- If capturing requires a degree of relaxed openness, composing is a little more closed.
- It can sometimes thrive on stress and adrenaline, although flow, getting stuff done, can feel great.
- There tends to be a definite purpose and objective in mind; like producing a finished product. One generally doesn't edit for the sake of it.
- The decisions you take tend to be structural rather than expressive.

When writing up notes into an email, you're probably less concerned with coming up with the ideas to talk about (these are already contained within the notes) than the order in which they are to occur, the words to use and the way the recipient will receive them.

Whenever you compose reports or theses, write up emails or process notes you should treat yourself as an editor and select your tools accordingly.

WHAT TO DO

DIFFERENT TOOLS HAVE DIFFERENT STRENGTHS

There are clear differences between information methods. They can be described according to two properties: entropy and abstraction. What does this mean?

Entropy has a few meanings but here I'm using it to describe the amount of disorder within a system. That is, how much information an entry method can produce. A pen can make any two-dimensional shape while a keyboard can only make one of a few different characters.

Abstraction is more, well, abstract. I could describe it to mean the amount of learned behaviours a piece of information must be forced through before you can get it out of your brain. It is easiest to understand it as the opposite of "intuitiveness".

Let's look at a few common information tools in these terms:

HANDWRITING

The pen requires no bothersome change of mode to scribble a diagram or mark-up with arrows, squiggles and scores. Compared with touch-typing, writing by hand is slow. Using a pen can even hurt - ask anyone who's recently taken a law or history exam! The effort and time that goes into handwriting makes it scarce; it's not that easy to produce. An economist might say that the handwritten word is more expensive than the typed word.

With a pen, the writer forms words in a similar way to an artist forming an image. Words are constructed by the creation of individual letterforms on a page. In cursive handwriting, the letters combine together in a pattern. In this respect, the pen is closer to a painter's brush than a typist's keyboard. Indeed, word forms tend to be more fluid the more often you write them. Compare your signature with a rarely-written word. The latter is more deliberate and probably takes a little longer to write. This is important because handwriting forces the writer to have a direct relationship with the word, just like speech. You might find that handwriting feels closer to the act of speaking, as though the pen somehow has a better connection to your brain - it's the most intuitive way to physically represent words. You might find that you come up with better ideas when handwriting. Perhaps this is why.

KEYBOARD

Typing is different. It creates far less entropy than handwriting because the writer only has a choice of 95 or so characters per keystroke. It also requires much less effort to form letters, particularly for someone who can touch-type. A typed letter is also identical to another of its kind. The writer doesn't need to care about strokes being made. The keyboard is also faster, easier and less painful than the pen. This shifts the emphasis of a writer's relationship from the letter to the word.

Typed letters are cheap, so words become disposable. They may be restructured at will. Whole sections of text may be reordered or rewritten without any need to damage the page as would be necessary when changing a handwritten document. Typing allows you to experiment, to find what sounds best without having to get it right first time. It may be that "cut", "copy", "paste", "delete" and "undo" may have had as big an effect on writing as the development of the alphabet and the mass production of paper. It seems that these benefits come at the expense of the intimate connection your brain has with your hand while writing. It's a far more abstract activity than handwriting. Typing is an unnatural skill to learn but you must also learn how to deal with the computer and operate the application you're typing in. It's best described as manipulating information, not making information. When typing, I feel I am being less creative, but more precise. I come up with better structures, more accurate language and a sense of how my writing flows as an argument.

SPEECH

In some ways, speech is the most extreme information-generation method you use. It's as close as you can get to connecting your brain with the outside world and the information it creates is rich and expressive. To start with, it's fast. A fast typist can produce 80-90 words per minute but this is glacial in comparison with normal conversational speech, which is almost double that. Speech is innate. Maybe you've found yourself coming up with your very best ideas when having a conversation, or perhaps you're sometimes criticized for not thinking before you speak. You might have hit upon a great way to tap into the brain's ability to produce ideas.

Taking these two points together means that speech can contain lots of rubbish as well as lots of great ideas. As long as you're recording it, that's no bad thing since you can separate useful information from rubbish later on. Spoken words are ephemeral - gone as soon as they're spoken except in the (volatile) memories of those within earshot. In a different way to handwritten words, spoken words are acutely scarce. To record your voice in an affordable and portable tool is a very new phenomenon, so not everyone is comfortable speaking out their notes. But it can be useful in situations that require the extremely fast capture of lots of information.

MIND MAPS

Something like mind mapping is unlikely to be completely alien to you because most people will have used something like it already, in school or at work. I dread to think of the hours I've wasted in tortuous brainstorming sessions where ideas are excreted onto white boards and flipcharts. It's a shame. Mind mapping can be a very enjoyable and productive experience.

A mind map is a cascade of information. It will usually begin with a single, central word or phrase, called a node. Branching off from this are child nodes, often with children of their own. This is important because the relationship between nodes, say, parent - child, aunt - child, cousin - cousin, sister - sister, describes the relationship between different pieces of information. For example, sister nodes might each contain a series of different points, while their children explore the detail of their parents. Digital mind mapping tools allow you to shuffle nodes around, promoting, demoting and altering the structure. This malleability makes it easy to deconstruct and reconstruct ideas and arguments, or even merge ideas together.

Mind mapping lends itself well to short pieces of text rather than massive chunks. The best mind maps have nodes that are rarely longer than a sentence. This is great for speed of entry and clarity. The sentence is a useful "atom" of information. Consider using a subject, verb, object clause. It contains enough material to make sense on its own, but not so much that it creates a structure itself. The mind map should represent the structure in information, not the nodes.

As a consequence, mind maps are useful for capturing sophisticated information. While they encourage you to avoid waffling, they also make it easy to understand the relationship between those ideas. This means that you can move from a collection of simple ideas to forming a logical structure. This could involve the key points of an argument for a piece of writing, a business plan or project.

OUTLINES

Outlines and mind maps are closely-related. Both forms symbolize a cascade of information. The only difference is one of presentation, but this means they can be used for different purposes. Each method of presenting the information has advantages. For example, because a mind map is so visual it makes it easier to understand a complicated, non-linear structure while one tends to read an outline in a more linear top-down manner. It's more intuitive to shuffle nodes around on a mind map (although this is still much easier with an outline than a word processor). An outline looks more like a traditional list or text document with points indented and outdented to show the relationship between them. Outlines are best for bigger chunks of structured information where nodes require more detail. This is particularly useful when writing a long document.

It's possible to begin composing an idea with a mind map, then to expand upon it using an outline. In this way, you can create of the document and capture the key points which it must contain. Mind maps and outlines can share the same file format making it easy to move from one to the other. Converting from a mind map into an outline will make it easy to add lots of fine detail.

Outlines have one final trick up their sleeve. They can contain more than one column. This is useful when comparing two different series of points, say, two arguments that disagree, or two characters in a play. The columns can also be handy for applying detailed markup such as dates, checkboxes, and star-ratings.

DOODLING

Doodling is innate; certainly far more innate than typing. Children learn to scribble and doodle around the same time that they learn to speak. One of the big advantages of doodling is speed. I suppose there is some truth in the adage "a picture tells a thousand words"; it's certainly faster to sketch out an idea than to write a thousand words to describe it! Notes might be combined with doodles to illustrate and annotate a concept. In this way, a lot of information, a lot of meaning, can be captured in a short space of time.

It is especially effective when information density is very high, time-dependent (as is the case for a conference or a film) or unstructured (such as a meeting or a conversation). You can dart about the scribble instantly, absorb visual, auditory or emotional information and dive into as much or little detail as needed.

When doodling, you don't need to force information through layers of learned behaviours, as is the case with typing or mind mapping. This low abstraction means that you're thinking more about the subject than the scribble.

MATCH THE RIGHT TOOL TO THE JOB

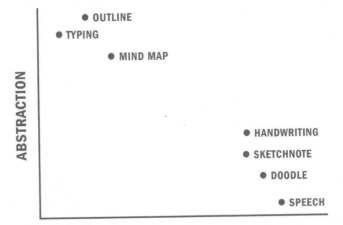

Note how the methods form two distinct clusters: analogue and digital.

ANALOGUE

Analogue methods are better at stimulating ideas. Why do these diverse and individual forms of creativity share this property? It's a hard question to answer but it makes sense to look at what they have in common.

Time flows in one direction using these methods. It's relatively hard to go back in time and erase a handwritten word to start again. The spoken word is the ultimate example of a high-entropy, low-abstraction. A word, once uttered, is utterly ephemeral and without technological help cannot be captured or manipulated at all.

Tools that fall into this cluster correspond well with the open mode.

DIGITAL

Digital methods free you from having to think about the letter. Instead they allow you to focus on the word, the structure of the sentence and the construction of the work. It's easier to step back and go backwards and forwards in time too. They're non-linear, meaning they allow you to build documents from an outline or restructure them. In addition, they can prompt you apply a more rigorous standard of logic and to structure to your work. These methods are more appropriate when writing up or analyzing your work.

This cluster is a good fit for the closed mode.

THE RIGHT TOOL FOR THE JOB

You might like to invest some time in finding methods in both clusters with which you're comfortable.

When any piece of information requires a certain standard of finish, something to be edited into a coherent piece of work and shared with another person, it's a clue that a digital method is needed. This gives you the freedom to take structural editing decisions without being hindered by the preciousness of the words as they exist in your notes.

When taking notes or just looking for inspiration, analogue methods could help tune your brain to synthesize better information. It's worth investing in a notebook for meetings or the library, or installing a voice recorder app on your phone when out on a run.

This distinction lends itself to a technique which solves a fundamental problem of software task systems. As digital tools they (correctly) lend themselves to quick decision-making, edits and deletions. But often, information is captured in environments which better suit the open mode of creativity, and therefore, analogue tools. Try using an analogue tool to capture intentions and tasks when in those environments. For example, you might like to record your voice when exercising, or buy a waterproof notepad to use in the shower. Crucially, those notes must be captured in your task system. It's best to do this quickly so that you avoid undermining the benefit of using a single bucket, described in *Habit 1: Capture*.

TWO-STEP WORKING

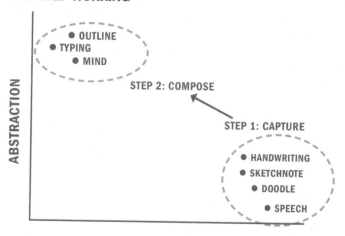

ENTROPY

By becoming aware of different qualities of the ways ideas are generated, you can string them together into a workflow that maximizes the brain's natural talent for connecting and creating information, and its talent for structuring it into something that makes sense.

You shouldn't have to decide to use only one method of generating information, it's better to take advantage of the benefits of both clusters. You can ease the production of great ideas by using entropy and abstraction as guides for finding the right tool for the job. The two clusters implies a workflow of two steps; first extracting information from the head, then turning it into work.

Busy events, conversations and moments of inspiration are situations which are dense in information and they generally don't allow you to go back in time and review points. A method of capturing information is required. When forming ideas, taking notes or just looking for inspiration, the analogue methods could help you synthesize better information.

Composing a finished piece of work or turning this information into a meaningful structure needs more discipline. Digital methods are best for taking those ideas and editing them into coherent pieces of finished work, whether writing up ideas into a document or creating an outline, plan or strategy.

WRITING UP

I've described how analogue tools can be used as the first step of a two-step capture method. It's critical to be consistent in placing all information into the capture system (the second step), otherwise you risk using lots of different capture methods and juggling them all.

A regular rhythm of review is the best way to do this. You can use your processing triggers for this. For example, schedule five minutes after every meeting to extract any tasks from your notes and place them into your capture system.

You can use a useful trick to make this easy, yet produce incredibly rich information. You may have notes captured during a meeting or some kind of creative session. These could be text-only, doodles, or a mixture of text, doodles and diagrams marking up the page. They could be a set of voice recordings (or even photographs).

Write them up in the form of an outline or mind map. This will allow you to preserve the structure which might have already been defined, or allow you to build a new structure. Mind maps are particularly good for this as they represent, visually, the logical flow of an discussion, argument or idea. They can be restructured visually, augmented with additional notes. They can even be merged with other mind maps.

WHAT YOU GAIN

A HEIGHTENED AWARENESS OF THE WAY
YOU CREATE INFORMATION

You might already have had a feeling that your tools affect your thinking. I hope these concepts have helped you to make sense of that feeling.

It can be rare these days to have a conversation about, for instance, handwriting, without someone talking about how it is "dying", presumably implying that the pen is being replaced by the keyboard. I don't think this is the case. Handwriting and its related information methods are at their most useful when capturing and creating information. Since these jobs are as crucial as they've ever been, it follows that handwriting is equally crucial. This system provides a framework for identifying information methods, and a principle for deciding when to use them. This forces you to be aware of the two attention "modes" - an open mode for creating ideas, and a closed mode for executing and polishing them.

In addition, you have created a distance between these activities. For example, you can eradicate the burden of editing at the same moment as creating. This will give you the freedom to engage better with whatever you're doing. After all, it doesn't matter that I can't dictate a finished, edited script into a voice recorder. Better to relax and come up with witty lines of dialogue and plot points which I can write up later. You can then begin having more fun with your tools since analogue tools are better for play and experimentation, while digital tools like mind maps and outlines are great for structuring and polishing, without the pressure of coming up with new ideas.

BETTER QUALITY OF IDEAS

Once you distinguish between analogue and digital methods, you could find your tools induce you not only to produce more information, but better information. For example, carrying around a notebook, voice recorder, camera or whatever is appropriate to the situation you are in will encourage you to take advantage of your linguistic and visual faculties because of the open mode they can stimulate.

Routing this information into your capture system makes it subject to the same processing habit as everything else. This means you have the added benefit of knowing that high-quality ideas are to be the subject of high-quality decision making.

Similarly, better notes will lead to stronger editing decisions because you've encouraged yourself to enter a more disciplined mode where your job is not to create, but to cut and compose.

This habit might raise hackles. It double-enters information and forces you to spend extra time thinking about your tools. Both of these would seem to violate common sense principles about productivity, which suggest that you should be more concerned with "doing" than with set-up work. It seems counter-productive. However, you're not really duplicating information. It is true that you might type up the same words you've handwritten, but by decoupling the open and closed modes, you're undertaking two entirely different tasks, each at the appropriate time, rather than forcing yourself to attempt both, simultaneously. It should become clear quite quickly that the quality of your work will improve. This will make the habit easier to pick up over time.

A CONSTRAINT

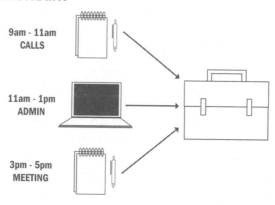

9am - 11am
CALLS

11am - 1pm
ADMIN

3pm - 5pm
MEETING

When you think about the open and closed modes of attention you'll notice two interesting effects. The first effect relates to planning your work. The ability to deduce from your schedule the tools you'll need for the day is common sense. However, you can now look at your calendar or schedule and judge the mode you'll be in. This means you can forecast the nature of the information you'll be producing. For example, if your schedule contains a lot of meetings or lectures, but little time to write up and process that information, you'll be able to pre-empt a lot of stress by adjusting your schedule in advance.

The second effect relates to the way you can make sensible decisions about the work you can do, based on the availability of your tools. With a big list of tasks to do, but only a notebook to hand, you know to focus only on those tasks which you're in the

best position to deal with right now - analogue notes, for instance. Or if you're in a café with your computer you know to put your headphones on and get down to compiling notes into a coherent document. The availability of tools constrains your choice of what to do. This is a surprisingly powerful effect because it makes it easier to choose, and therefore begin,
tasks right now.

SOMETHING TO CROSS OUT

Once of the most useful things about this habit is that it will give you something to get rid of. By writing up notes into a finished piece of work or extracting tasks from voice recordings and images, then placing them in the capture system, you can cross out or dispose of the original note. The scrunched up bits of paper and strikethroughs in a notebook are a physical proof that things are getting done. This can give you a very real sense of progress and completion. This is a powerful reward which will drive this and many other productivity habits.

Exploring this in more detail, you will have the satisfaction of knowing that you've dealt with the information correctly, especially if you're using an analogue method as a kind of vacuum cleaner, collecting information into the capture system. Crossing out the notes at this point removes the ambiguity of storing information in lots of places. If captured notes are consistently written-up, the habit will become very easy to maintain because it can compound the positive feelings associated with the capture habit.

KEY POINTS

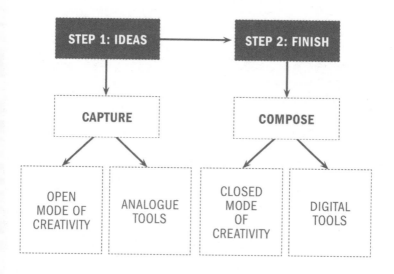

SITUATION

CONTEXT, DEFINED

THAT WHICH ENABLES AND CONSTRAINS

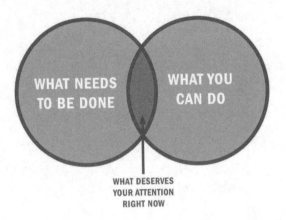

WHAT NEEDS TO BE DONE

WHAT YOU CAN DO

WHAT DESERVES YOUR ATTENTION RIGHT NOW

Think about how the situations in your life enable and constrain you. I want to set out some principles to help you understand how these situations relate to one another, plus how they relate to what you can be doing, and what you should be doing.

Traditional methods of managing tasks, of10 rely on the idea of priority as the main way of deciding what to do. This is unsatisfactory. Priority is really a binary idea - that "this" is the only thing in the world you should be doing right now.

I of10 see the old sliding scale idea of priority being used to decide the order in which tasks should be completed. That's fine for children whose homework 10ds to come at them like items on a conveyor belt. But modern information work is different. Instead of a conveyor belt, messages and tasks arrive out-of-order and at10tion skips between lots of different strands that run in parallel (and sometimes collide).

It is better to consider what can be done right now, based on the current situation. Out of all of the things that could be done, you should decide what should be done. If you can get into the habit of making this choice based on your situation, you'll be making a big leap from efficiency to effectiveness. It will help you to make better use of your time and respond appropriately when both free time and emergencies appear.

Your situation consists of at least one context; that is, an environment which allows certain things to be done.

ARE CONTEXTS RELEVANT?

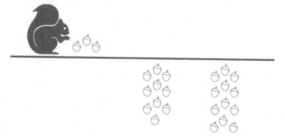

Back in the early 2000's, when *Getting Things Done* started to make an impact, it was easier to define "context" as far as information work was concerned. For most people, a computer was something that sat on a desk. There was an actual difference between "online" and "offline". Contexts could be defined by the availability of tools and resources alone. These were my contexts from 2006:

- Home
- Computer: Online
- Computer: Offline
- Phone
- Cafe

- Library
- Supermarket
- Book shop
- Bus
- Train

This system failed for me. Sometimes I'd have 10 minutes at the café, other times I'd be able to brood for hours over my coffee. I might have been able to deeply focus at the library in the morning, but distractible and inat10tive after lunch. My contexts are more than just locations and physical objects. Besides, technology is making the boundary between physical locations more fluid. I can be as equally "online" on the train as at the desk. I do my weekly grocery shopping using an app on my smartphone, email from the bus and consume articles and books as audio while at the gym. You could partake in video conferencing from the bath if you wanted to, although the author accepts no liability for loss of property, reputation or livelihood if you're stupid enough to try it.

So is there any point thinking about these exclusive constraints when these very constraints are breaking down? On the contrary, I believe that contexts are more important than they've ever been. The growing ambiguity about the work you can do has increased the need for clear divisions which show when certain kinds of work are more appropriate than others. It doesn't seem right, as technology becomes more powerful and more friendly, that we must slog away harder, longer and dumber. Clear situational distinctions help me to say "no, I shan't do this", rather than "no, I can't do this". This is a level of control which is quite realistic but it requires two stages:

- Greater situational awareness, which is to say a study of the circumstances in life that could define a context. It's important to understand precisely how these circumstances affect the nature of your work.

- Quick recall of what you can do, in any situation.

THE CONTEXT TRIANGLE

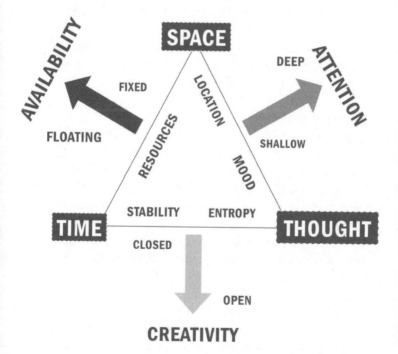

First, I want to establish a sensible definition of context that will allow you to understand how they relate to each other and how they differ.

A context is some particular instance of space, time and thought. Think of them as the points on a triangle with lines connecting them. This is what happens on those lines:

TIME AND SPACE

Space and time both define the resources to hand. They describe the **availability** of a context. For example, an ex10ded period of time, writing with your notebook and reference material to hand could be described as a high-availability context. But when interviewing a busy expert, you're in a low-availability context. Time and space also define whether the context is fixed or floating. That is to say, do you need to be at "a" bank, or "the" bank? These are very different environments where different activities need to happen. You can deposit a cheque at any branch of your bank, but you need to be at a specific location to meet the bank manager.

SPACE AND THOUGHT

Space and thought determine the kind of **at10tion** that a context can accommodate. I of10 find that I work on different projects in different places. I find that I simply can't work at home at all. It's a location that lends itself better to low at10tion tasks and quick reviews of information. I have to go to a library or cafe to do anything serious. Your mood will also relate to the kind of work you want to do. Whether you are feeling good or feeling low, combined with the suitability of the location, strongly influence the nature of the at10tion you can give to a task or project.

THOUGHT AND TIME

The time you can spend in an environment is greatly affected by its stability. Frequent disruptions break a large block of time into smaller pieces and this affects your creative mode. An stable block of uninterrupted time is wonderful for the open mode. The variation in the information being worked upon - entropy - is also extremely important. A playful, conversational, "corkscrew" activity is likely to involve a greater variety of information than more anxious, focused thinking. Together, stability and entropy combine to determine your kind of **creativity**; whether that is the open mode or the closed mode.

TRIGGERS

WHAT TO LOOK FOR

Think about your different instances of space, time and thought. What are the implications of these situations on your availability, attention and creativity?

EXAMPLES

For example, your time might be divided into small chunks between phone calls, and big chunks in your study or on a train. In some situations you might feel open, conversational and creative. In others you might feel more closed and decisive. There might be general locations like a bank where you have quick, "brain dead" stuff to do. But at "the" bank, meaning one specific bank, there might be more intense meetings to have.

The context triangle is a mechanism for interpreting all the situations you find yourself in. It will form the basis of a taxonomy of contexts.

It might not be necessary for you to apply the full detail of the context triangle - people tend to feel relief at the control the triangle gives them or a little nervous because of its complexity. If you're one of the latter, don't worry. Your needs will depend upon your workload, your flexibility and your ability to immediately judge what you should be doing. If you don't need to consider your emotional state before working, or if you can produce equally good work no matter where you are, you can adjust your set of contexts accordingly. And if you're not sure whether you need every feature in the context triangle, start easy.

Analyze your past week, and your week ahead.

To begin constructing your context taxonomy think back to all
the different situations of space, time and thought in which you
found yourself during in the past week. Consider the following
factors for each:

LOCATION
- Did the situation feel tied to, or defined, by the location?
- How did the location affect your mood?

MOOD
- Were you feeling positive or negative about yourself?
- Were you feeling good about what you were doing?
- Did the work feel like something you wanted to do?
- Were you relaxed and social, or closed and pressured?

ENTROPY
- Consider the environment. You might find that information-rich
  environments like libraries, gardens, cafés and galleries support
  the open mode of creativity while blander, information-poor
  environments are better suited to the closed mode where you
  don't need too much external stimulation.

STABILITY
- Was the environment a refuge from distraction?
- Were you likely to get called away?
- Were there lots of potential disturbances from people or things?

RESOURCES
- What tools did you have available?
- Did you have, or need, supporting information or any other
  objects in order to work?
- Were there any time constraints?

Unique combinations of these various factors create a context, in much the same way that the dials on an amp allow a guitarist to create a particular sound. They are the mechanism by which a context can effect the kind of work you can do. If you list them, it could be enlightening to see the sheer number of different environments in which you find yourself. Consider how the factors that make up each context can effect the kind of things you can do in the context. When you compile this list there might be obvious gaps for you. The context triangle gives you a principle for filling them.

IN A NEW SITUATION

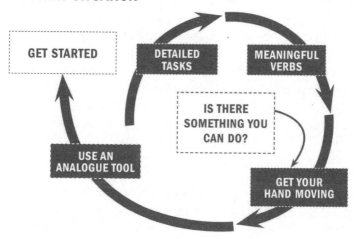

Procrastination has always been a huge problem for me. Even when writing this book I'd plan to spend an hour in a café or at my desk, only to waste half of it browsing the web. I'd know that it was a waste of time and I'd end up regretting it, but I'd find it perversely difficult to start working. And, of course, with 20 or 30 minutes before my next appointment I'd panic and begin working, only to be forced to stop just as I'd reached a state of flow. This is an ongoing struggle for me; perhaps you've experienced something similar. It's easy to fall into the fake work trap. When sitting down at the desk or on the train or waiting in a queue, it's tempting to start fiddling with emails or compulsively checking Twitter.

I'm especially vulnerable to distraction when entering new situations. I get stuck in a feedback loop of fake work which becomes harder and harder to break, ruining a wonderful opportunity to get stuff done. This can be particularly pronounced after a productive day or having to do something that requires willpower. Willpower is a finite resource and once the day's supply has been exhausted, it can be especially hard to get started.

There are a number of strategies you can employ to defeat this:

GET THE HAND MOVING
Turning the hand to some physical creative action is very effective. For example, handwriting random rubbish, or doing a mental sweep for a few moments so that you create words on paper creates a sense of flow which you can then turn to a task.

ANALOGUE TOOLS
Analogue information methods like sketching or handwriting tend to involve more physical movement than digital methods. Low abstraction tasks tend to reduce the amount of effort required to create information. This makes it easier to begin working.

DETAILED TASKS
When tasks contain all, or at least a good amount, of the supporting information you'll need to complete them, you won't need to dig through reference materials or original notes to make sense of them. The verb, subject, object method I described earlier is extremely

effective but there's no harm in attaching more detailed information if needed.

None of these strategies is perfect; like anything difficult, willpower is required. However, they all require a certain amount of situational awareness which I will show you how to systematize over the next few sections.

MEANINGFUL VERBS

When writing out tasks and choosing the verbs to assign to an intention, it's perfectly valid to use "begin" and "continue". These are useful because they do not imply a sense of completion, making it acceptable to only write a few words. Any progress is good progress. These verbs make it easier to started because you don't need to worry about finishing. Odds are, however, once you get into a creative flow you'll produce more work than you might have imagined.

WHAT TO DO
CONSTRUCT A TAXONOMY OF CONTEXTS

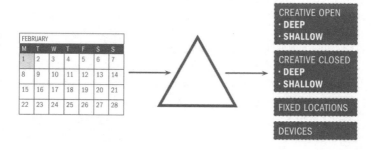

A taxonomy of contexts is a map of your lifestyle.

It's important to build a context system which works for the situations in which you find yourself. The context triangle can guide you to build this structure. This is important because the structure should reflect your situations, lifestyle and the constraints these place upon you. It's also important to consider how you'll actually use them. For example, when walking into a cafe, you may find that several contexts apply and so you should be able to recall more than one. Because of this, the structure should really be a taxonomy; that is, an ordered classification which explains how each context relates to another and provides a logical way of summoning up the appropriate context for any situation.

A decent task manager tool will let you build perspectives or views constructed of several contexts. Those that rely upon tags should be able to create saved searches which retrieve multiple tags. A situation should trigger you to review a particular perspective. That perspective will contain multiple contexts. Take a look at your list of contexts from when you analyzed your past week. Remember that these are like little bubbles of space, time and thought which enable particular kinds of work, and make others more difficult.

I like to divide my taxonomy into three branches: creative, floating and meta.

CREATIVE
The situations where creative work - both capturing and composing - can occur often blend into each other. Some kinds of work can be performed both in the office and on the train. Other types of work are best left to one or the other of these situations. When you're sitting on the train, your situation has already been defined. Out of all the work that is available for you to do, it's the level of attention and creativity it requires that defines whether you should do it.

HOW TO REFLECT THIS?

I like to start with the open and closed modes of creativity. This is great for loosely breaking down different situations into the kind of creativity that they'll facilitate. Combine this with attention. Attention can be deep or shallow, and tasks that rely on deep attention in the open mode (such as writing a section of a thesis) are totally different to tasks that rely on shallow attention in the same mode (for example, sketching a diagram or fleshing out an idea).

You now have the dials you can turn to define your creative situations. These contexts will combine together in interesting ways, according to the situation you're in. Interestingly, your creative situations tend to occur in fixed environments: the study, the café, the office, and so on. These are independent situations which can share some kinds of work.

- A perspective that reflects the situation "train" or "on the go" can consist of closed - shallow and open – shallow.
- The "study" situation could consist of closed - deep, open - deep, open - shallow contexts.
- "Café" could suit open - shallow and closed - shallow contexts.

FLOATING

These situations are totally different. They comprise mutually-exclusive contexts in which the actions you can perform in one typically cannot be performed in another. You wouldn't do your grocery shopping in the post office or clean the bathroom in your local bookshop. It makes sense to group your "opportunistic" contexts together. However, while these situations are more specific than creative situations, they are less fussy about where they occur. You can buy dinner at any supermarket.

There are tasks, usually sundry items, which require a particular tool. Consider creating a "devices" perspective for your computer, phone, tablet and camera. This is less important because the more significant activities belong along the creative branch, but it can still be useful for maintenance tasks.

META

Sometimes, tasks reference or spawn other tasks, making them meta. You'll find that, for some tasks, certain events need to occur in order for the task to come alive. Sometimes you'll delegate stuff to other people and create a task to chase them up. Some tasks will depend upon a future event before they can become active. "Chase client for payment on October 12th" can belong in a "waiting for" context, and set to become due by a certain date, if the client doesn't pay. "Buy a new table when client pays" can sit in a "holding pattern" context, to be prompted whenever the event occurs. "Discuss tardy payments with client when we meet" is a task that could belong in an "agendas" context, to be looked at when preparing a meeting.

Create a "considerations" perspective to show all of these meta contexts. It's useful to monitor this perspective fairly often, perhaps when you conduct your morning review.

This taxonomy is useful because it clearly defines the relationship between situation and context. If it seems a bit too finicky, don't worry. The beauty of perspectives is that you probably won't need that many of them. If in doubt, err towards simplicity. A single "study" perspective is all you'll need unless you happen to work in a library. However, it is important to construct the perspectives carefully, because when you refer to these, you'll want to see the relevant contexts.

DEFER TASKS

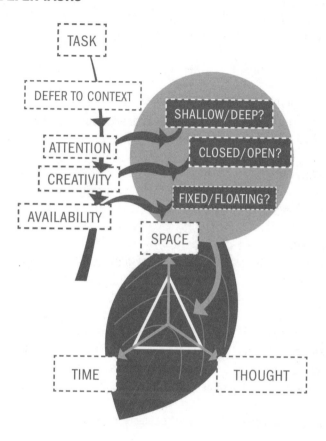

Memes become intentions when they trigger ideas. Intentions become tasks when you add a verb. Tasks become actions when they are deferred to a future situation where they can be done.

Now you've constructed your taxonomy of contexts you need to hang your tasks from it. This will occur at the defer stage of processing captured information, when you will throw tasks into the future using your task system. You should consider how and where they land. The context triangle is a useful guide.

Consider these three factors and how your tasks are effected by them:

AVAILABILITY
- Does the task require a particular location or set of resources, or can it occur anywhere?

CREATIVITY
- Does it suit the open or closed mode of creativity?
- How long will the task take?

ATTENTION
- How much mental or physical energy would you like to invest in the task?
- How much care does the task deserve?

These questions can apply to any task. The context triangle lets you relate them back to the attributes of space, time and thought that govern the distinctions between your contexts. This will make it easy to choose the right context for your tasks.

Your task manager should have a category for contexts or let you add a tag by context.

When you enter a particular situation you'll just need to review the perspective in which you find yourself. This becomes a task list which is completely appropriate to the situation, listing the one or more contexts that have become available to you. It should be easy to begin working straight off this list.

WHAT YOU GAIN

MAKES A TASK DOABLE

A result of this habit is that you gain a great deal of control over the circumstances that lead to certain kinds of work. By categorizing your tasks according to this taxonomy you'll be able to instantly know what you can do, whenever and wherever you are, and however you're feeling, without having to sort through a long list and remake decisions about each item/an unambiguous list of what you can do right now.

In a sense (and you may see a theme beginning to emerge in this book) you've constructed a mechanism for taking advantage of thinking you've already done. By adding a verb to an intention, you created a task. By adding a context to a task it becomes an *action*. These are important distinctions because at each step you add meaning and reduce the amount of set-up work and friction. As a result, when you find yourself in a new situation you can begin working immediately and, since the act of beginning is a significant part of the challenge facing people who want to work, the impact on your productivity could be significant.

MAKE SENSE OF PRIORITY

Priorities only make sense when they represent the one thing in the universe to which you should be saying "yes". The priority of a particular action is irrelevant if you're in a context which doesn't allow you to deal with it. But of course, you are thinking about it. And if your idea of priority owes itself to the ABC list, you might have multiple "most important tasks" with which you're not in a position to deal right now. This can only create stress and a feeling of being always on the back foot. Adjust this definition of priority. What if, rather than being the most important thing you "should" be doing, you define it as the most important thing you "can" be doing? Here, priority becomes a fluid concept, providing a different answer depending on your context. It provides a rapidly-shifting focus, like *The Lord of the Rings'* "Eye of Sauron" that sweeps across your projects as you move from context-to-context. This lets you decide, easily and instinctively, what is the most important action with which you can deal right now, so helping you to engage properly with whatever situation you find yourself in.

SCHEDULE PLANNING

Just as your contexts structure allows you to shift your focus across your projects and priorities, you can shift the contexts themselves across your schedule. You can plan contexts in advance or adjust them as needed. This means that if something urgent comes up, or you've got large number of tasks sitting in a context which you won't be in for a long time, you can reconsider your schedule.

In this way, a calendar changes from being a rather clumsy way of organizing tasks to a much smarter "landscape", defining the events you must attend and also the conditions of space, time and thought which define the work which must, and can, occur. The implications of your contexts provide a tremendous amount of insight and power over your future schedule. If a situation has to be bumped to a later date because an urgent change must be made, you won't lose any information because the tasks are still assigned to their contexts, ready to be picked up when you need to look at them. As a result, when this habit develops, it can give you the ability to pre-empt last-minute panics.

A SENSE OF PROGRESS

9AM   10AM   11AM   12PM   1PM   2PM   3PM   4PM   5PM

You can take advantage of the craving for completion described in the processing habit. This new precision in your task list allows you to deal with the most important task in your situation, but the specific availability of other tasks makes it really easy to complete something you might not otherwise have started, if relegated to a lower priority. You will find that completing actions becomes somewhat automatic. You'll have the pleasure of ticking tasks off your list, but also of reducing the number of open actions you've committed to undertake. The context triangle can encourage you to consider other opportunities to work. These are often small gaps in your schedule, like five minutes over coffee or a few minutes waiting for an egg to boil. Normally the time and effort involved in finding, or thinking of, useful things to do, combined with the probable lack of a habit to prompt you to consider it, meant these moments were often wasted. But now it's possible to mine your time and availability for opportunities to do something useful. Consequently, you gain a sense of progress without effort and control without panic. This can make a surprisingly significant impact on the sheer amount of stuff that can be done, but more importantly, it frees up higher-quality time for more meaningful activities.

KEY POINTS

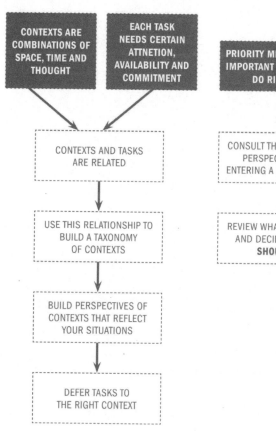

CONTEXTS ARE COMBINATIONS OF SPACE, TIME AND THOUGHT

EACH TASK NEEDS CERTAIN ATTNETION, AVAILABILITY AND COMMITMENT

CONTEXTS AND TASKS ARE RELATED

USE THIS RELATIONSHIP TO BUILD A TAXONOMY OF CONTEXTS

BUILD PERSPECTIVES OF CONTEXTS THAT REFLECT YOUR SITUATIONS

DEFER TASKS TO THE RIGHT CONTEXT

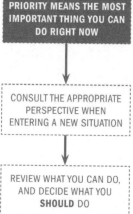

PRIORITY MEANS THE MOST IMPORTANT THING YOU CAN DO RIGHT NOW

CONSULT THE APPROPRIATE PERSPECTIVE WHEN ENTERING A NEW SITUATION

REVIEW WHAT YOU CAN DO, AND DECIDE WHAT YOU **SHOULD** DO

WORKING
MEMORY

TRIGGERS
WRITING OUT TASKS

Creative flow is sense of fulfilment when you accomplish something; a sense of momentum and progress that stimulates a very deep focus. You experience flow in the moment and it can exist in both the open and closed modes. These are moments when you get to exercise your mastery of yourself and the world around you - it's exhilarating, powerful and rather good fun!

Earlier, I described how properly written-out tasks provide supporting information. This is important because you shouldn't overthink when working. But it's possible to use actions to stimulate a sense of creative flow. A musician in a state of flow doesn't have to look up the next note mid-performance. Having to think - or overthink - can disrupt creative flow. The ideal task should require only the most basic level of thought, and provide enough information to get you into a state of flow.

Tasks tend not to be completed in a vacuum. Rather they advance a project, step-by-step as they are completed. Where is the boundary between a project and a task? Going for a 30 minute jog is, for an adult, something that can be executed with a single thought. A one-year-old child has to do a lot more thinking in order to toddle ten paces. A task for one person could be a project for someone else, meaning that the task contains too much information for the second person to complete in a single step. In this case, it requires too many discrete thoughts to complete. For example, "prepare business plan for meeting with investors" doesn't tell you how to begin, nor does it give you much supporting information. A project built out of this kind of task will require you to hold too much information in your head. On the other hand, a task could contain too much information. For instance, "pick up pen for taking notes" is quite obvious and doesn't tell you anything useful. A project consisting of anaemic little tasks like this will actually contain far too much information, and will slow you down. What's needed is balance; a sensible boundary between task and project to provide just the right amount of information to stimulate a creative flow.

PROJECTS AFFECT PEOPLE IN DIFFERENT WAYS

A project is an intention that requires two or more discrete tasks to complete.

It seems quite sensible to assume that a classical pianist is likely to make a better DJ than someone who's never touched an instrument - thought I'm sure there are exceptions. Similarly, a professional chef will master an unfamiliar recipe faster than someone who lives on baked beans and take-away pizza. You experiences and talents affect your ability to pick up certain kinds of projects. It's wise to consider your expertise in the kind of work you intend to do when writing tasks and planning projects. On paper, this seems mind-numbingly obvious but when beginning a project I've found that people often fail to consider their level of personal mastery. Be honest with yourself - have you written a business plan before? If you are not an experienced business coach, you might need to break this into smaller tasks.

WHAT TO DO

MEASURE WORKING MEMORY

As you experience and learn things, your mind compiles groups of information into "chunks" which can be recalled into working memory. These chunks are really cues to easily retrieve and unpack information, which has become internalized, and as you master an activity, those chunks automate the retrieval

of more and more information. Your working memory is a clear space in which ideas are expressed and manipulated.

You might be familiar with the psychologist George Miller's *"magical number 7 (±2)"* which refers to the span of human working memory, meaning the number of chunks you can accommodate in your working memory at one time. Psychologists have argued about the exact number and the degree to which it varies, and as I write this the neurological mechanism behind working memory remains unclear. However, it's clear that working memory can only handle a finite - and really rather small - number of chunks. It's possible to take advantage of this knowledge when building tasks and plans. A well-written task consists of a verb, subject and an object, and ideally each should be a discrete chunk, meaning an item or thought in your working memory. So at three chunks per task, it's easy to see why it's hard to think about more than two or three tasks at one time.

To extend the example of a business plan:

"Research competition for investor's business plan" is much more sensible. The verb is clearly defined and you probably know how to begin, since there are only three discrete thought to have in mind. If "research" isn't a single conscious thought for you, break up the task until you're working with three chunks at a time.

You can calibrate this idea by making sure that any tasks you undertake can be accomplished during one session in a particular context or situation. This way, you can terminate your creative flow with a feeling of completion.

USING GRAMMAR TO ESTABLISH YOUR IDEAL SIZE OF TASK

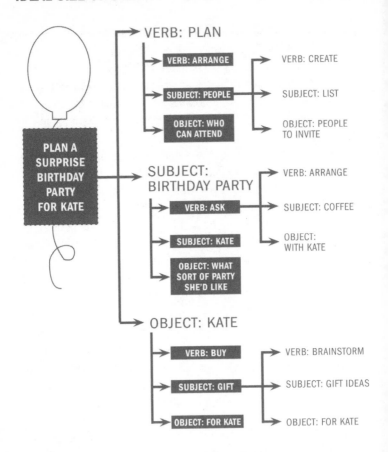

I want to demonstrate a simple method which you can use to break down a task which is so big that it doesn't mean much, into a series of tasks which contain just the right level of detail. This can help you to turn procrastination into creative flow. Your linguistic faculty offers a cheat. It's possible to use grammar to work out the size of task with which you're most comfortable. Language is inherent in the concept of an idea. Ideas and their constituent ideas may be expressed as proper sentences comprising a subject, verb and an object. The most basic form of a proper sentence is a subject - verb - object structure. It is the most minimal way of expressing some sort of proposition or a unit of conscious thought.

Subject: What you're talking about.
Verb: The action; the change; the operator.
Object: The end result or the context.

This is the most basic way of expressing any change, conjunction or separation.

The nice thing about these clauses is that they can be hooked on to each other. This is how you compose complex sentences, paragraphs and prose:

The cat (subject) sat (verb) on the mat (object) and slept (verb) until dinner (object).

Since tasks are more about demanding some sort of change rather than making a statement, they take the form of verb - subject - object. But these can also be hooked together:

- Pour vodka, Cointreau, cranberry and lime juice into a cocktail shaker
- Shake the mixture with ice
- Strain the mixture into a martini glass
- Slice a piece of orange peel
- Flame the peel with a match
- Garnish the cocktail with the burnt peel

CASCADE

Sentences are recursive, meaning that you can write sentences about sentences. You can take advantage of this.

- Write out one of your projects as a proper sentence comprising verb, subject and object elements.
- Then write a verb, subject and object for each of those three elements.
- Repeat this process until your sentences describe no more than three discrete thoughts, or one per sentence element.

This process creates a cascade of information. Here's an example:
Project: Plan a surprise birthday party for Kate

This creates three meaningful sub projects:

- Arrange people who can attend
- Ask Kate what sort of party she'd like
- Buy a present for Kate

...containing specific, well-defined tasks.

You might be surprised at the sheer amount of information you were having to hold in your head when working on the project. This method lets you get it out of your head and define what means.

DEFER THE TASKS

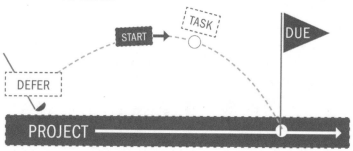

Each of the tasks you've created should fit neatly into one of your new contexts. How you do this will depend on your preferred system for managing tasks. Most decent task management apps will let you assign project and context attributes to a task in the form of categories or tags. This way, you can associate a task with the project it will advance and the context where it can be actioned. Hour-on-hour you'll be working across your projects horizontally as you move from context-to-context. Defining a project as a sequence will also let you move up and down your projects, vertically. This will become very useful later.

What about dates? It's extremely helpful to throw tasks into the future and I don't want you to lose that. Similarly, some tasks should only become available when a preceding task is complete. A software tool should enable you to define a date on which you'll be reminded to do the task. Good task management systems allow you to specify a due date, by which time a task should be done, and a defer or start date when the task becomes available to begin. This lets you create a window of opportunity. It should also allow you to create a sequential project which will only make a task available if a preceding task has been ticked off.

WHAT YOU GAIN

THE OPTIMAL SIZE OF TASK

This exercise is powerful because of the remarkable self-awareness it can generate. It will give you an intuition for the best size of task to stimulate a feeling of flow when working, or at least to get you started. It will also show you where the boundary between a task and a project lies for you. Once this intuition exists, you'll naturally start creating tasks which fit your working memory. It's likely that you'll only need to repeat the process when you begin a project of a type that's unfamiliar to you. When working, each task will require just the right quantity of information so you won't need to interrupt yourself to dig through notes to make sense of what you're working on. The habit will also make it more likely that all your tasks will require only the right quantity of information.

Not having to keep a detailed plan in your mind will give you enough specificity to know precisely what to do right now. Notice how the verbs have become much more precise. This process will yield words like "sketch", "note", "handwrite", "research", "write-up" instead of the more general "do" or "work on". The verb contains more information about the action than the outcome. This precision lets you hold a smaller amount of information in your working memory. A project which comprises tasks like this won't require you to hold the whole project in your head to work on it. It'll also give you the freedom to focus deeply on what you should be doing. But the tasks also contain enough information that they add value. There's no need to externalize information that can be recalled by instinct or habit. You don't need your task list to remind you how to breathe.

BETTER QUALITY OF THINKING

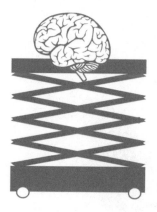

Earlier, you defined a precise taxonomy of contexts. Now you have a method for creating equally precise tasks. This combination can lead to some very powerful results. Since you've already considered the availability, attention and creativity required to turn a task into an action, you don't need do this in the moment of action. As a result, you can get started immediately.

When I first started applying this habit, I noticed I was getting less frustrated when working because there were fewer instances of knowing that my brain could do something I wanted to do right now, were I not in an unsuitable environment. Instead, I had a feeling of flow and a sense of being engaged with my situation since I could I start making use of that situation immediately. The combination of precise contexts and precise tasks creates what I like to call a decision-support system. The tasks and contexts are now good enough to enable you to spend your time making smart decisions and creating stuff, without having to take on the burden of remembering all the information required to support those decisions yourself.

PLANNING EVERYTHING IN ADVANCE?

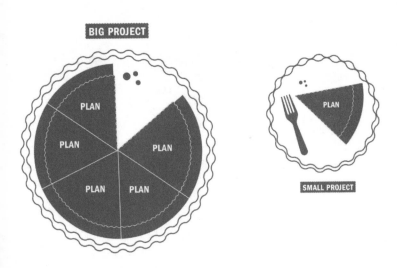

It could be tempting to imagine that this is a method you should use to plan the details of a project from beginning to completion. Certainly there are some projects where this is feasible:

- Planning a holiday
- Cooking a meal
- Arranging a meeting

But there are other projects where it is laborious, if not impossible, to plan the whole thing in advance:

- Researching a paper
- Writing a film
- Building a house

These are bigger, multi-phase projects with no implicit end. They are only finished when you decide they're finished. The information in these projects tends to bloom, or mushroom. For example, when researching the nature of working memory for this book, an answer to a particular question I might have could throw up ten more questions. I couldn't foresee these questions in advance. There was no way I could know every little detail to include in this book before starting. Some books just write themselves, and this can't be easily planned for. And, naturally, when working on a large project that involves other people, it's impossible to account for their foibles and delays. These projects can have predictable milestones, which you can map out in advance, but you shouldn't worry about having to plan these down to the last detail. For now, awareness of your working memory, and the cascade method, are tools to help you get started.

KEY POINTS

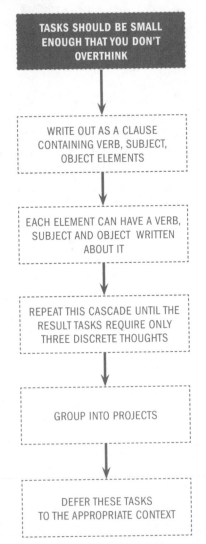

TASKS SHOULD BE SMALL ENOUGH THAT YOU DON'T OVERTHINK

WRITE OUT AS A CLAUSE CONTAINING VERB, SUBJECT, OBJECT ELEMENTS

EACH ELEMENT CAN HAVE A VERB, SUBJECT AND OBJECT WRITTEN ABOUT IT

REPEAT THIS CASCADE UNTIL THE RESULT TASKS REQUIRE ONLY THREE DISCRETE THOUGHTS

GROUP INTO PROJECTS

DEFER THESE TASKS TO THE APPROPRIATE CONTEXT

PLANNING

TRIGGERS

PROJECTS AND COMMITMENTS

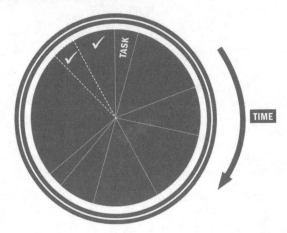

Earlier, I described a project as an intention that requires at least two steps - two tasks - to complete. I find the word "project" often puts people off, what with its implication of Byzantine plans, cost and time overruns, late nights and bad coffee. I prefer to think of a project as a convenient way to throw - to project - some goal into the future, and use its constituent tasks to reach that goal. It could have two tasks or two hundred. You'll probably face much larger projects than the focused examples I gave earlier - bake a cake; write a report, and the like. These are the fiendishly complicated activities that require a lot of advance planning.

Examples could include big goals like:

- Start a business
- Write a novel
- Find a new career

Unlike small projects and tasks, these are deep goals that require care and commitment to complete.

This presents two challenges:

- How to focus on these commitments when it feels that the world is conspiring to keep you too busy.
- How to plan them, which is to say, how to turn a life-long goal into the next ten minutes of your life. You need to throw - project - this information into the future in such a way that it'll make sense when you come to work on it.

You could become functionally productive but it doesn't mean anything if you're not working on stuff that you care about.

Several years ago, I found myself in a job which was extremely challenging and, at the beginning, intellectually-engaging. But I found myself getting bored very quickly. After a few months, I began to despise my alarm clock. Perhaps you've had a similar experience. I didn't exactly hate the job but I certainly didn't love it. I suppose I tolerated it for over a year which led to my becoming depressed and uninterested. Eventually I realized I was wasting my time because *I didn't care about what I was doing.*

When presented with a list of projects and significant objectives, I've found that most people are very good at deciding which of them is the most important. However, this rarely translates into action. You might know that the work which takes up most of your time is not that important, but it takes up all that time nonetheless. This problem often manifests itself as boredom at work or a feeling of wasted potential. It's cognitive dissonance. Perhaps you've experienced it? It's not within the scope of the book solve this problem magically, but I'd like you to consider that feeling as a trigger for a set of processes which will help to analyze the issue and provide a set of tools to help you decide on more meaningful work. If you think what you're doing - productively or otherwise - isn't what you really care about, then this could well be a good habit to adopt.

WHAT TO DO

UNCOVERING THINGS YOU CARE ABOUT

There is a very interesting relationship between your immediate needs and your later wants, or objectives. A need is predicated by a want; and a want is important because it is really just a deeper need.

Take one of your tasks. Something you need to do. Try to find the "wants" that underpin this need. This is a very effective way of probing and analyzing yourself, teasing out the things that drive you. You'll find that needs and wants are connected by a thread, and that thread is importance. As you go deeper, you might discover profound aspects of yourself which underpin the things you do. For example, tasks and projects exist to support deeper commitments, but these themselves are based upon cares, passions and loves that form the core of your character. Someone of a more spiritual inclination than me might say that these are the reasons why you're on the planet.

1. I need to clear the floor because I want a tidy flat.
2. I need a tidy flat because I want to impress my partner.
3. I need to impress my partner because I want a serious relationship with her.
4. I need a serious relationship with my partner because I love her.

1. I need to buy a pen because I want to write today.
2. I need to write today because I want to finish chapter eight.
3. I need to finish chapter eight because I want to write a novel.
4. I need to write a novel because I want to be an author.
5. I need to be an author because I want to tell interesting stories.
6. I need to tell interesting stories because these are things that I love.

These "cares" are not really intentions; they are more like descriptions of your personality; aspects of yourself that have accreted in your character because of your experiences. They do not imply a sense of progress in themselves, rather they draw intentions toward them, like planets orbiting a star or branches growing out of the trunk of a tree. Since this tree is connected together by importance, I'll describe this relationship an *"importance tree"*, the structure and content of which is utterly unique to you.

How do you know that the trunk of the tree - your cares - has been reached? Cares don't behave in the same way as the intentions which branch from them because they are like aesthetic judgements. They are subjective preferences which imply no sense of progress. As you go deeper and deeper into the tree, if what you find implies a sense of progress, some sense of difference between the way things are now and the way you'd like things to be, then you need to go deeper.

MAP YOURSELF

"...we must make the goal conform to the individual, rather than make the individual conform to the goal." - Hunter S. Thompson

Try to repeat the want-need process with the rest of your tasks. You'll find that the process is exploratory, and it will feel like creating a map of your own head. A mind map is particularly helpful for this because it can represent a tree-like structure. You may uncover several paths when mapping yourself. They should all lead back, eventually, to things about which you care most, which define you. It may be that, by this point, you'll have uncovered a small number of deep "cares". If that's the case for you, great. However, your need-want steps may lead back to a large number of cares. You might consider each member of your family, or your best friends, to each be a discrete "care" but this, alongside the other things you care about, will quickly become unwieldy. It would be impossible for me to tell you that a certain number is too many, of course. It might be tempting to try to find something which underpins the love you have for your children - "I wish to ensure the propagation of my genome" - but this doesn't seem like conscious "caring" to me. And you might be reluctant to tell yourself that your love for your family is really a means to some material end.

No, I think it makes more sense to consider each "care" to be a facet of your character. I consider my family and friends to live within the same facet; and therefore, they represent one "care". Remember that this map is a guide to your own sense of what is important. It is not a promise to others, so you shouldn't feel guilty because you haven't inscribed particular names onto the trunk of your "importance tree". By now, you should have identified at least some of these cares, these facets of your character and the structure of your "importance tree" as it is right now. When I first performed this exercise, I found it interesting that my "importance tree" had fallen into place without any planning. After all, this was the first time in my life that I'd achieved this kind of overarching view and I was impressed that a structure of considerable sophistication had emerged without any design. However, my decision-quality being what it was, many aspects of my life were pretty badly planned: a job I didn't enjoy with an escape plan that wasn't going to work; creative pursuits that had no real direction. Perhaps you feel the same. Shortly, you'll use the map as the basis of a better-designed plan for your commitments and projects.

GROWING BRANCHES

A task advances a project, a project gives progress to a commitment, and so forth, all the way back to the goals which satisfy your deepest cares as a person.

By now, you've mapped your deepest "cares". I hope it was an illuminating process for you. It's important now to work outwards from the trunk of the "importance tree", validating your existing commitments if they deserve it, and build new commitments which will feel important to you. I call these the "big nouns" because they are the polar opposite of the precise little verbs you started using in *Habit 5: Working Memory*. These big nouns are the largest branches that connect to the trunk of the importance tree. They may be written as the sentence, "I am a...":

- "I am a parent."
- "I am a dancer."
- "I am a campaigner."

These nouns denote the activities which outwardly define you. The problem is, they are often elusive. Asking someone to summon up life-long vocations on the spot is - understandably - a tough request. The problem of finding something to do which will fulfil you is familiar to anyone who's had to apply for a new job, a new course, or deal with a career advisor. It's a complicated problem which, as yet, I haven't found a way to solve for everyone. However, there are a couple of techniques which are helpful. First, try conjoining your cares. For instance, you might love literature and you might love science. Big nouns might emerge from the synthesis of these cares:

- Science fiction author
- Scientific communicator
- Science editor

It's possible to use the need-want technique to add additional clarity to this process:

"I need art so I want to be an illustrator."

Be cautious when you do this. Needs tend to derive from a single want, but a single want can create many needs. You'll probably find yourself creating dozens of big nouns. This is good. If you don't, the second technique could help: a brain dump. Just as you might capture your tasks, try writing a list of your current major commitments and big projects. The need-want technique will let you trace back to your cares via the big nouns in between. Take note of them. The big nouns will tend to be occupational. But all of them will relate back to something about which you care deeply.

The next step is to process them. Go through each in turn and decide whether you actually want to pursue them. This "yes/no" decision-making process functions in a similar fashion to the task review in *Habit 2: Processing:* it's a form of quality control. It will allow you to evaluate your current vocations as well as help you choose new ones. The decision could involve considerations such as your well-being, financial viability or whether your talent for the particular noun matches your ambition. Now that you have this information you should be able to brainstorm areas of responsibility, like careers, hobbies or areas of interest.

The next level out could contain commitments, which in turn drive projects and tasks. All of these levels are intimately related, in the same way that leaves, twigs, and branches relate to the trunk of a tree. To be able to express this relationship between the smallest action is incredibly powerful. It's a great way to organize your life and to gain an over-arching view over what you're doing with your life. In a sense, it's a visual representation of your future autobiography. But you're not done yet. You've expressed the relationship between your deep cares, down to your commitments. It's necessary now to examine how projects are planned, down to the tasks.

CASCADE PLANNING

In *Habit 5: Working memory*, I introduced the concept of the verb-subject-object cascade. An intention can be written as a sentence containing a verb, subject and object. Each of these elements may, in turn, have a verb, subject and object written about them. It's a very effective algorithm for turning a task which contains too little information into a project comprising well-written and meaningful tasks. These technique is useful once you've established commitments and projects, to turn them into doable tasks.

By now you should have an idea of why certain projects matter to you, how to create them, order them and to begin them. I want to hang the project described in Habit 5: Working Memory (plan a surprise birthday party for Kate) from the "importance tree". This should demonstrate the power of a well-planned project as it relates to a deep care.

These tasks are all connected by a thread of importance to the reason someone might be on the planet. I've also noted the contexts that each task relates to.

THE FIRST STEP

The order created in your project now requires a first step. This initial task is very important because it will help prevent you from overthinking the overall objective of the project, which cannot yet be grasped. A clear first step will help prevent you becoming overwhelmed by the feeling of "too much to do" when starting out. Instead, consider the next thing which must happen which will bring you closer to your goal. This will become much easier now that the project has been clearly written-out as ordered small tasks. If you're stuck, try working backwards from the first item in the cascade. Now, refer to the cascade. Derive a first step for each sub-project. This will make it easy to progress throughout the project. It's difficult to use this process to build an entire project plan, but you don't need to plot everything in advance. When beginning a project, it's important to create a sense of a momentum and direction; you'll be able to flesh out the plan as you go.

RELEVANCE AND URGENCY

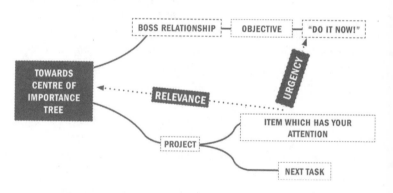

Urgency is just disorderly relevance.

You may notice some commitments and projects appear inherently more important than others. The importance tree provides a system for understanding this, but first you should ask the question: "What is importance?" It sounds like a simple question but the answer turns out to be rather interesting.

Importance is one of the factors which determines how you should treat different channels of communication, alongside volume. This can be broken down further. A communication can be relevant (meaning it relates to something you care about) and/or urgent, meaning that bad things could happen if it's not dealt with in time.

RELEVANCE

Means the strength of connection to the larger commitment, and ultimately the passion that underpins it. It is a pull that runs straight up the importance tree. To say that something is more relevant means that it has a better connection to something you care about.

URGENCY

A leaf on a tree can be pulled by its parent branch, but occasionally it might be disrupted by its aunt. When something is pulled sideways on the tree, it is urgent. A time-critical request from the boss to buy him his lunch is not likely to be directly relevant to something I care about, but it is urgent because I want to afford my home (so I need to keep my job, and keep the boss happy).

"I need to breathe because I want to live."

Both relevance and urgency combine to determine importance. This principle applies to any form of communication where you might find intentions. Understanding this can help you to be aware of where your cognitive dissonance comes from. When you spend too much time responding to urgencies, it might indicate that you could be doing something more relevant.

WHAT YOU GAIN

WORKING ON STUFF YOU CARE ABOUT

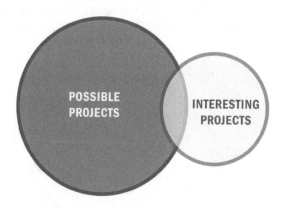

The importance tree links the very next thing you'll do, to the reason for you to be on the planet. This gives you a system for finding things to do that you care about. For example, rather than trying out new creative pursuits in a relatively unguided way, you can target specific areas of interest. You might know that you love space and storytelling, so a course on sci-fi writing or science journalism would be likely to pique your interest.

Once these commitments have been identified, the importance tree can help to plan projects which contain specific tasks. As a result you can take deep, esoteric knowledge of your character as well as your ambitions and turn them into something actionable. In addition you can find gaps in your activities.

If you have several cares but your activities only reflect one or two of them then there is an opportunity to find activities which are relevant to the other cares; maybe even replacing the least relevant activities in your life. This question - "do I care?" is profound when working with the importance tree. You can decide whether your existing activities adequately reflect your cares. Your day job might be too far-removed from your cares, which could either be a prompt for change or a justification for saying "no, because I don't care".

A SENSE OF CONTROL

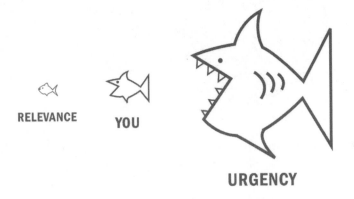

RELEVANCE   **YOU**

URGENCY

It's important to understand why something is urgent. The importance tree is a system which models the difference. Being overly responsive to urgencies that keep popping up, like "whack-a-moles", is a sign that there is a conflict between relevance and urgency. On the importance tree this means that something you care about is frequently disrupted by another branch. If this happens too often, it is a sign that something is wrong. If there are too many conflicts between relevance and urgency you might decide to change direction in order to find new occupations or lifestyles where there is harmony between things that matter and things you care about.

The importance tree allows relevance and urgency to be considered together, and so it becomes a system for deciding what should be worked on as well as what can be worked on. This decision expresses the relative importance of the task. When in working situations, you can look at a task and see the project associated with it. Having expressed the relationship between that project and why you're on the planet, you might find yourself innately judging its importance. Importance also makes it easier to plan to work in the future.

A daily review of tasks - consulting the importance tree - will let you to defer the urgent tasks to appropriate contexts, but find relevant tasks to work on too. Instead of always feeling that you're on the back foot by responding to an onslaught of pressing-but-irrelevant tasks, you can gain a feeling of proactivity by working on the tasks which mean the most to you. By being aware of what makes your work important, you can have some control over it. It's rather like having your hand on the tiller of a boat.

KEY POINTS

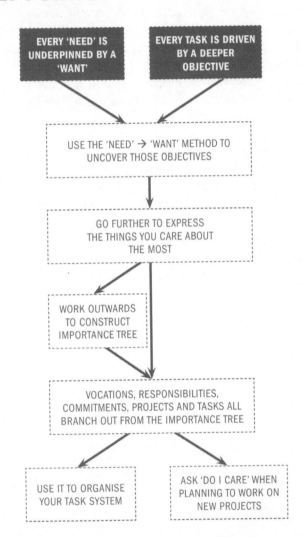

EVERY 'NEED' IS UNDERPINNED BY A 'WANT'

EVERY TASK IS DRIVEN BY A DEEPER OBJECTIVE

USE THE 'NEED' → 'WANT' METHOD TO UNCOVER THOSE OBJECTIVES

GO FURTHER TO EXPRESS THE THINGS YOU CARE ABOUT THE MOST

WORK OUTWARDS TO CONSTRUCT IMPORTANCE TREE

VOCATIONS, RESPONSIBILITIES, COMMITMENTS, PROJECTS AND TASKS ALL BRANCH OUT FROM THE IMPORTANCE TREE

USE IT TO ORGANISE YOUR TASK SYSTEM

ASK 'DO I CARE' WHEN PLANNING TO WORK ON NEW PROJECTS

ARCHIVING

TRIGGERS

CAPTURED INFORMATION THAT NEEDN'T
BE ACTED ON OR DEFERRED

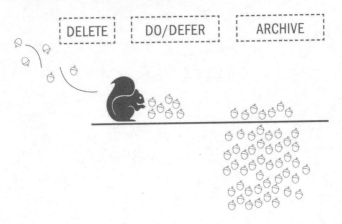

Consider the processing habit - a list of unprocessed tasks and a
very simple vocabulary of verbs to apply to them:

- Delete
- Archive
- Do
- Defer

The only one I haven't addressed so far is "archive". I've noticed that
people often neglect to get into the habit of using a good archiving
process, even once their tasks are under control. I think archiving
is very important. You might often have ideas, notes or pieces of
information that don't necessarily imply a specific intention, but
you'd still like to keep them. Some examples:

- Good ideas that cannot be acted on right now
- "Someday" projects and commitments
- Specific notes for a future project
- Mementos which stimulate an important memory
- Correspondence to keep for reference
- Finished work

Without dealing with this properly, this material can build up and make a mess, reducing capacity to work. When archived information is treated as actionable it creates a glut of unnecessary tasks; a form of information overload. I classify material to be archived in two categories:

- Something which should be retained for an unknown reason
- Reference material for a known future project

Active tasks are relatively easy to handle because, by their very nature, they are incomplete. By looking at them, the objective is obvious and the intention is immediately meaningful. You might say that these tasks and the information to which they relate are "alive". Material to be archived will also have an objective - either explicitly known or implied - but it is not immediately meaningful. The thing which unites any item in an archive is that it is essentially "complete"; that is, that there is no immediately meaningful objective you should be working towards right now. But this does not mean that the information is "dead". In that case there would be no objective whatsoever and therefore it should be deleted.

I consider complete work by you, and complete work by others to be in the same category here. As far as an archive is concerned, there's not much difference. Your work-in-progress is a completely different entity from the sources of information that feed into it. When the "product" is complete, it becomes just another potential input for a future product. The fact that you were the author just means that you - or your past self - was a person you happen to know quite well! Archived material is alive, but in a different way to incomplete information. It's alive, but unconscious. It isn't needed yet, but it could be. In the future, it might wake up and require action. It might. This uncertainty triggers a new process that runs alongside, but separate to the task system.

RETRIEVAL OF ARCHIVED INFORMATION

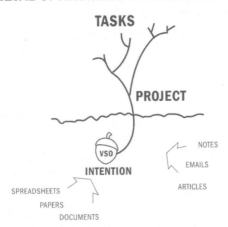

On of the most interesting things about information in an archive, is that it removes the distinction between types of information. While you're working on them, the difference between an email, a handwritten note or a sketch is quite plain and useful. These differences should inform your choice of tool or app, even the appropriate context. These differences all rely on the information being alive and conscious, as they are only relevant as "incomplete" moves to "complete".

When you create a piece of work, the kind of work matters a lot.

You would treat a document different to a spreadsheet, an image, or a message when you're creating them. These distinctions evaporate in an archive. Or at least, they should. "Dormant" information may be relevant to a current or future project, but that relevance won't care about the file extension! The information must be sorted together, equally, into one place where it is easy to find. When tasks are extracted even emails should become dormant and unconscious. Draining the immediate intentions from emails removes their psychic pull.

WHAT TO DO

BUILD AN INFO DUMP

IMPORTANCE TREE

BIG NOUNS

AREAS OF
RESPONSIBILITY

INFO DUMP

What's needed is a single place to store unconscious information. It's sensible to apply some of the same principles used in the capture habit:

- Use a single tool to consolidate information.
- Don't be overly concerned with quality control.
- Route different channels of data into the archive.
  Use it to archive emails, along with web links, text chats and meaningful photos.

The process of archiving is less about creating information than making quick decisions about what goes and what comes out. This system requires an environment that lends itself to quick decision-making. Digital archiving and knowledge management tools are best. I like to call this an "info dump" because the act of just dumping stuff into an electronic bucket is far easier than burying something away in a complicated filing system. This begs the question - how to organize the info dump? Is it even worth organizing it at all? To answer that question, consider that the info dump is really a kind of external long-term memory. Its job is to balance the two conflicting needs of easy storage and easy retrieval. It is easy enough to archive information in a system that is literally just a bucket without any sorting, but it is quite difficult to draw useful information from it.

It may be tempting, in the first flashes of excitement after starting out with a new tool, to pre-empt yourself and create some fantastically complicated structure of folders or tags or labels, or whatever organizational signpost the system gives you. It's like scaffolding - necessary, but only to a point. It's important not to go overboard with it. A good filing system should let you archive something correctly and retrieve it in seconds. If you have to think hard about where to put it, or where it might be, then it's too complex. The importance tree - the structure which relates your cares and commitments to your projects and actions - is a good guide for how to structure the info dump. You can begin the structure or labels around your big nouns, or areas of responsibility. When information starts to flood these categories so that retrieving it becomes unwieldy, consider branching out, creating subcategories that reflect commitments and projects.Some of the most complicated projects work in phases. For example, these are the phases I've been through to write this book:

- Research and planning
- Write first draft
- Polish final draft
- Editing
- Publication

Each of these activities is quite different and I've archived information which is specific to each one. This will be similar for most large projects, like starting a business or building a house. If your info dump tool has a tagging mechanism, you might like to create tags for each phase so that you can quickly pull out material relevant to whatever phase your project is in.

DUMPING STUFF

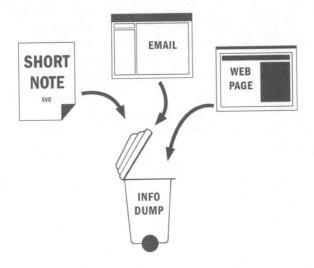

It's best to minimize the amount of effort required to archive something into the info dump. This will make it easy to build the habit and reduce the friction associated with its day-to-day use. A good time to drop stuff into the info dump is when you're processing your list of captured ideas and tasks. Emails and other forms of communication can be archived periodically as well. Just as with tasks, the two-minute rule is a great rule-of-thumb to ensure you don't get too bogged down. Make sure that archiving an item takes no longer than two minutes. When archiving is fast-paced it can give you a feeling of progress and completion, not to mention that getting through simple work like this can be fun.

Different sorts of information might require different levels of support information as they go in the archive. Text notes and images can benefit from a short sentence - even a subject, verb, object clause - summarizing their point. Longer documents, articles and web pages will tend to contain all the information necessary to retrieve them, although a summary sentence that can be read in a hurry certainly won't hurt. Similarly, emails contain all the information you'll need to retrieve them in their metadata: sender, date, subject. Since most tend to be fairly short you shouldn't need to go to any extra trouble summarizing each message. Just import them directly to your information dump.

The data in the info dump represents the concentration of a vast amount of useful information which cannot be easily replicated. This makes it valuable. As a result, it's worth spending time to make sure it is always safe and backed-up. The best back-up strategies comprise a copy of the data, kept up-to-date on-site, and another copy kept up-to-date at another location. This way, it's easy and quick to recover from a system failure or accident, but you also have a safety net in case of flood, fire or theft.

RETRIEVAL OF INFORMATION

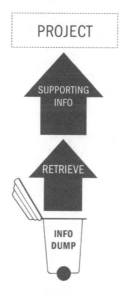

When you begin a new project or look for ways to make progress on something that you've already started, it's a good time to consult the info dump. Depending on the system you're using, you could search, drill down into the filing structure, or some combination of the two. The most advanced knowledge management systems can even produce a dossier of information which relates to what you're doing.

This information can be treated as new input. It can stimulate new ideas and intentions which can be captured by turning them into written tasks, or incorporating them into plans for a current project. This is extremely effective for when starting to work on commitments which comprise lots of small projects. In writing this book, I've collected thousands of items of research. When beginning each new component of a new habit I'll search my info dump. Information will then appear; old notes alongside emails, outlines, articles, scanned documents and photographs. This all helps to inform my plan for the book.

WHAT YOU GAIN

A RICH SOURCE OF SUPPORTING INFORMATION

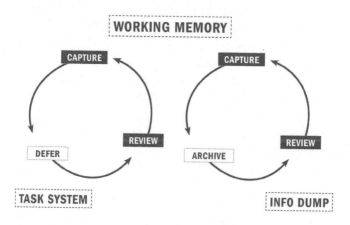

With one place to store and refer to, archiving becomes easier and habitual which will mean you'll use the info dump more often. By getting into the habit of using it, you have created a form of external long-term memory and a method for using it seamlessly with your task system. It will do a better job than your brain at remembering, and the info dump encourages the growth of cognitive hyperlinks. Is it a good thing to trust technology with such a critical part of your cognition? I can certainly see why it might be a cause of discomfort but with the amount of information in our lives, I think it's fairly inevitable. These are some of my anecdotal observations after embracing this process:

- I invest less effort learning useless information, and more effort internalizing information which means the most. As a result, I've become much better at the skills and specialisms which matter the most to me.

- It's become easier to relax about the fate of good ideas; a relief to know they're safe.
- I'm preserving far more detailed information in the info dump than my memory could ever cope with.
- Referring to external sources for information has become habitual. This increases the reliability of that information.
- A premium has been placed on the critical thinking skills needed to evaluate sources, and compare and analyze different sources of information. I've become much more conscious of the importance of the channels of information which feed into the capture system and info dump.
- I've become far more vulnerable to losing data caused by damage or loss to my equipment. I strongly urge you to consider backing up your info dump.

The archive is a kind of external memory in which every piece of information has been pre-judged to be interesting in some way. As a result, the more stuff that goes in, the more useful it will become for new projects and commitments. This seems to be the opposite to the way most filing systems behave. It has the effect of bringing my past work, and that of others, to bear on current projects; and focusing it to an acutely high relevance. There is also a sense in which the info dump allows information to evolve. Consider that your complete work becomes input for new work, which in turn becomes relevant reference material. It's a cycle that generates new information.

KEY POINTS

"DO I CARE?" IMPLIES THAT INFORMATION CAN BE DEAD, ALIVE OR UNCONSCIOUS

↓

UNCONSCIOUS INFORMATION NEEDS TO BE ARCHIVED

IN AN ARCHIVE, THE TYPE OF INFORMATION IS IRRELEVANT

↓

BUILD AN INFO DUMP WHERE YOU CAN FILE ALL KINDS OF INFO TOGETHER

↓

AS INFO DUMP GROWS, CREATE A FILING SYSTEM BASED ON IMPORTANCE TREE

↓

REFER TO INFO DUMP WHEN PLANNING A NEW PROJECT OR COMMITMENT

REVIEW AND
COMPLETION

TRIGGERS

SHIFTING FOCUS

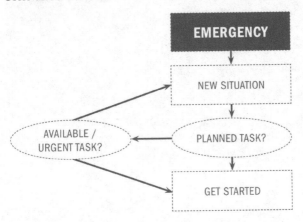

It's important to consider the day-by-day triggers to which you'll hook the routines of the system:

- Arriving in new situations
- Leaving those situations
- Travelling between appointments and situations
- Interruptions and notifications; signalling catastrophes or opportunities
- New ideas that come to mind
- Beginning a new project
- Down time at the end of a tough day
- Dead time between events or conversations
- Unexpected free time that you can gain through greater productivity
- Major life events that force you to re-evaluate the things which matter the most

Some of these triggers can be planned in advance, for example, putting your appointments or events into a calendar, and planning the commitments which fit into them. Other triggers cannot be known or planned for. Emergencies, by definition, are never known until they land. How you respond to these emergencies will determine how well you interact with a world that will often throw a grenade at you.

If you find out that a loved one is in hospital, you probably don't need to waste time putting that information into a task system. However, if your habits have given you the mental capacity to deal with the emergency, you'll be less likely to fall apart and your response will be all the more appropriate. By shifting focus to deal with a catastrophe or an opportunity, and shifting back to deal with something else, you'll have gained a whole new measure of effectiveness.

REVIEWS

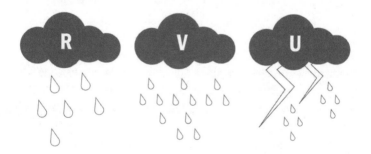

Information Theory, a concept described by Claude Shannon in 1948, forms the basis of modern computing and electronic communication. It also underpins developments in fields as diverse as neuroscience, linguistics and genetics, and ought to be as well-known as the theory of evolution.

WHAT IS A REVIEW?

To review information, in the sense that I am interested in here, is the process of thinking about information. This could be a long and deep process, like reading a book. Or it could be quick, like working through emails or choosing something to do from a task list. Looking at information seeds your working memory, which may catalyze a decision. This adds meaning to information, such as adding verbs to intentions in order to turn them into tasks. It's possible to treat any source of input, such as communications, reading material, previous work, conversations; even the task system itself, as a "channel". It is the review of your channels which provides motion and progress. I even consider my own mind, with ideas and thoughts bubbling out of my subconscious into my attention, to be a channel.

HOW OFTEN SHOULD EACH CHANNEL BE REVIEWED?

A channel is a means of transmitting an information signal. It's commonly used to describe methods of sending data in telecommunications and computing, but the principle can relate to any form of communication. That's why it's relevant here.

A channel - a form of changing information - may be analyzed using a simple method that draws from information theory, called sampling. If you want to record a musician digitally, you must convert the soundwave into a series of values, each of which represents the wave at a particular point in time. Together, those values allow the waveform to be reconstructed. Likewise, the more often you can take a measurement - the sampling rate - the more accurate the recording will be. Of course, music is complicated with lots of rich sounds so the more information you can capture with each sample - the resolution - the better the quality of the recording.

A similar principle can apply here to decide when and how to sample a channel.

RELEVANCE, VOLUME, URGENCY

The relationship between relevance, volume and urgency is useful here, and not just because it forms a convenient acronym "RVU".

- The relevance of a channel can be used to decide the resolution a particular channel requires when reviewed. This could relate to the resources you want to give it, whether that is time or attention.
- Volume partly defines how often the channel ought to be reviewed, in that high-volume channels should be checked less often. Less frequent batch processing of a lot of items is far more efficient that piecemeal fire-fighting.
- On the other hand, the more urgent a channel, the more often you should check it.

This conflict between volume and urgency is interesting because it implies that a high volume; high urgency channel is hard to deal with appropriately. As described in *Habit 1: Capture*, it's best to divide it into at least two channels, low volume; high urgency, and high volume; low urgency. The nature of urgency is interesting too because it defines the difference between checking the channel often, and letting it become a distraction.

To let something notify or distract you is to say that the channel deserves more attention than whatever you're working on right now. This kind of permission should not be given lightly. Something which is primarily relevant can also be urgent; this is to say that something you care about right now deserves a fast response. This should lead to a high sampling rate, meaning that you should check the channel often. For example, if you have diabetes or high blood pressure, it's worth checking your stats frequently. Channels which deliver low relevance urgencies - say the text messages from your boss ordering a sandwich - should be allowed to notify, disturb and distract you.

SITUATIONS AND REVIEWS

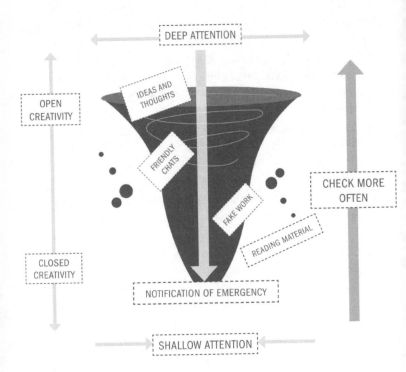

The events which trigger your reviews are intimately related to your situations. I want to show you how those situations relate to the relevance, volume and urgency of those reviews. The RVU concept, which defines the nature of any review, can be mapped onto to the context triangle. This will help you to match your situation to the kind of review you can perform.

RELEVANCE
You'll probably commit more easily to a book or film that you really enjoy - therefore, highly relevant - than to a bunch of emails or social

media feeds. This just means that you're giving more attention to one review than another. The context triangle indicates that your location and mood will affect your ability to provide deep attention. This is an important consideration.

When you're feeling pensive and sitting in a park, perhaps it'd be better to get lost in a good book than a dating app. You probably don't treat low relevance channels such as your work newsletter or utility bills (note the difference between relevance and urgency) with the same amount of care. These channels require shallower attention to review. It's also likely that those reviews aren't tied to a specific location, especially since the technology exists to access these channels almost anywhere.

VOLUME AND URGENCY

The frequency with which you check a channel is related to urgency divided by volume. High volume, low urgency reviews such as typical "fake work" (processing your emails or your captured task list), don't have to happen that often. These activities require relatively little stability but greater focus, suggesting that the closed mode of creativity is more appropriate. On the other hand, exchanging conversational messages with your friends doesn't occur quite so often. This needs very little focus but a certain measure of environmental stability. This implies that the open mode of creativity is better for that activity.

NOTIFICATIONS

I know that this is quite a finicky process, but I found that it provides a very important insight into the way my situations affect the quality of my work. I particularly like the fact that it can be used to make sense of notifications. Remember that you should only grant the privilege of disturbing you to channels that contain urgent information. A message from the boss, a family emergency; that sort of thing.

When a notification arrives it exerts a kind of psychic pull on your attention, fuelled by the strong possibility that it contains some unknown emergency. This makes it hard to remain focused on what you're doing - your attention is shifted to the incoming piece of information. Depending on the particular urgency, the amount of stuff - the entropy - of the information in your mind can be greatly reduced. This creates a moment of instability, during which you will switch to the closed mode. Perhaps this is why I find it difficult to be playfully creative when I keep getting interrupted! Your mood might also affect the sudden rise in attention, and it can feel overwhelming. By being aware of your mood when urgent information comes at you, you can make better decisions about how to deal with it.

WHAT TO DO

DO:

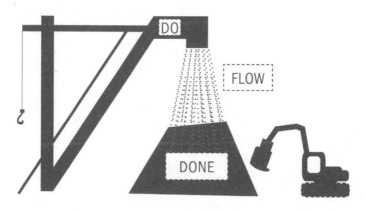

Up to this point, everything in the book has set you up for the act of doing whatever it is that you want to do. Consider this:

- All of your tasks should now be written out meaningfully
- They are assigned to a suitable context
- They are part of a well-conceived and planned project
- You can describe the importance of the project
- All supporting information is present

If these statements are true, you have created a very powerful and effective decision-support system. Now you just need to use it. When you enter a particular situation, take a look at the perspective which relates to it. Remember that your perspectives are unique collections of contexts which you can tailor to anticipated situations. This should show you all of the tasks that are assigned to the contexts in those perspectives. All of those tasks can be performed in this situation.

You can now choose the one to work on first. You may have already decided this in advance, perhaps as daily commitments. Or you might find yourself with a little extra time on your hands and look for something productive to do. Either way, you can now get to work. By setting up the tasks as you have, you won't have to do any extra thinking which can create friction and slow you down. You should simply be able to complete the tasks and tick them off. This should encourage a feeling of flow, that you not just an efficient machine but an effective human being.

CAPTURE

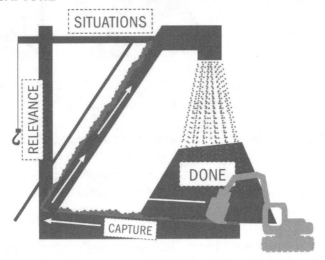

When working, it's likely that you'll generate a lot of new information. This could take many different forms:

- Complete work
- Follow-up tasks that relate to the work you've just finished
- Ideas that go off at a tangent from what you were doing,

sparked off from the various pieces of information in your attention as you work

Complete work can be fed back into your system as new input. For example, once compiled or shared, a project can be archived so that it can become a reference for some future piece of work. You might also use several steps to work on different parts of a problem. For example, if you're writing a paper, you may start by handwriting some notes or thoughts. Once complete, you could capture a new task to write up those notes, an activity that is likely to occur in a different situation. In this case, and for random ideas, it's especially important to have your capture mechanism on hand whenever you work. This way, if an idea comes to mind, you can get it out of your mind before it is lost and before it distracts you from what you're meant to be doing.

MAINTENANCE

This productivity system works on the principle of getting information out of your head. But that point is lost if the information is forgotten about or grows stale. That's when you risk losing control of your channels. A cycle of reviews prevents this by ensuring you look at all of your channels with an appropriate depth and frequency, making sensible decisions as you go. I'll describe a few different reviews, what to do, and how to describe them using the RVU concept.

SITUATIONAL REVIEW

This review involves looking at your available tasks, say, in a perspective of contexts, in order to decide what to work on. This review will help you decide what to do, so it's very important. The task list isn't likely to change more than a few times a day. But it can contain urgent information. This implies that it should be checked often; ideally when entering and leaving a situation. The relevance of the daily task list is less than that of the actual work you'll be doing, so you shouldn't have to focus too hard on the task list itself.

DAILY COMMIT REVIEW

Every day - the morning is a good time - take a look at all of the tasks you could do, based on the situations you'll be in. Mark or flag those to which you can commit to doing. This might be because a particular task is urgent, or simply because it's worth doing. Every morning you might plan out the day or the week ahead according to the landscape of situations on a calendar, or adjust that landscape to deal with important work. This can involve checking for tasks that are due or urgent today, or those which have become available because a preceding task has been completed. You could choose to review your available tasks and decide which of them you can commit to doing today.

The quantity of information to review is moderate (the entire list of available tasks), as is the urgency of the information. This supports the idea that, as a daily review, it doesn't need to occur quite as often as the situational review which occurs multiple times a day. However, the relevance of the information you're looking at is high, so it deserves a little more attention than a quick glance.

I found this review tough to get into at first because it needed me to use a little more discipline in the morning than I was accustomed to, not least getting up a little earlier! There are lots of silly hacks you can employ to help with this. My personal favourite is setting the alarm not for when I want to wake up, but for when I ought to go to bed. To be on the safe side, drinking two big glasses of water before going to bed is almost certain to get me up on time.

PROJECT REVIEW

The weekly review is one of the most important concepts introduced in *Getting Things Done*. I suspect it's also one of the least used. Every week, look at all of your projects to ensure that they are current and in motion. It's helpful to make sure that projects are filed in the right place, especially if you represent your Importance Tree in the way your task system is organized. Make sure that every active project has a next action available or scheduled, and deferred to a context. It's also a good time to clear out projects which are complete or which won't be done. These should be archived or put on hold, or even added to a "someday/maybe" list in your info dump. This is a good time to look at the calendar for the week ahead and ensure that you've scheduling enough time for important tasks.

There's a lot more information to review here and it's all highly relevant. However, urgency at this point is generally quite low - emergencies tend to occur at the level of daily tasks, and you can often get away with a sub-optimal task system for a few days. Therefore, conducting this review every week feels about right. However, there may be times when your projects will create lots of urgencies so you might want to dial up the frequency of these reviews until things die down again. This will help to ensure that your system is clean, maintained and in shape.

LIFE REVIEWS

I've always found it useful to think about my direction in life every now and then. A periodic review of your life is an opportunity to evaluate what you really care about, and how to reflect that in the way in which you spend your time. You're operating near the trunk of your importance tree, dealing with information that relates to the things you care about the most and so relevance is extremely high. The volume of information is potentially quite large, while urgency is rather low (this is more about defining your future activities rather than dealing with your current commitments). Consequently, this review can occur quite rarely; perhaps annually or after a major life event. But take your time when you do as this can require a lot of focus.

WHAT YOU GAIN

WORKING IN CIRCLES

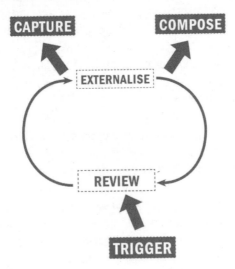

One of the interesting consequences of the Information Age is that knowledge, memory, thinking and creativity is increasingly less confined to the limits of a particular head. Instead, memory is becoming environmental and symbolic, particularly as you develop the habit of writing down and allowing much of your cognition to occur using tools, like the capture tool or the info dump.

Many of the processes in this book will appear to be quite similar. In fact, if you look at it a certain way it's just the same process applied on lots of different scales, from capturing small ideas to planning the biggest projects. That process is one which distills information from diluted, low relevance to concentrated high relevance by reviewing information, making small and fast decisions, then getting it out of your head. I assume that the brain is not an administrative organ but a creative and decisive tool. Externalize the stuff that your brain is not great at dealing with into external processes and technology. You can now begin to focus your brain on things that are meaningful without having to worry about making the wrong decisions or not having the right information to hand.

WORK ALGORITHMICALLY

The thing I most love about this process is that it turns the messy process of information work into a kind of mental algorithm; a step-by-step procedure for taking information in, adding meaning and producing some kind of output. But more than that, you've now got a process which digests the information in your life and work into an internally-consistent series of steps based on the idea of externalize, review; repeated over and over. It's a completely different way of dealing with information and it's very powerful.

WHAT DOES THIS GIVE YOU?

The first benefit is that the feeling of unclenching your mind, once relieved of its responsibility as a storage mechanism, can be become a normal feeling. Mastery and perspective, the two cornerstones of productivity, become habitual as a result. I've also found that working iteratively has given me much greater awareness of myself; not just the kind of stuff that I was holding in my head but also an awareness of what I'm capable of achieving at any given moment and how I respond to new information. There is also a profound sense of progress; the idea that even small steps turn big wheels; and the right wheels too.

A BETTER WAY TO HANDLE CHANNELS

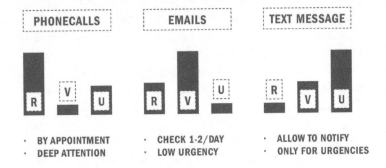

PHONECALLS
- BY APPOINTMENT
- DEEP ATTENTION

EMAILS
- CHECK 1-2/DAY
- LOW URGENCY

TEXT MESSAGE
- ALLOW TO NOTIFY
- ONLY FOR URGENCIES

One of the greatest difficulties you'll face is that, no matter how effective and efficient you become, no matter how sanitary your email habits, you'll have to deal with people who do not understand that it's wrong to expect a response to their "Urgent!!!" email twelve seconds after they sent it at 9pm, and the sales guy who buzzes your phone or turns up unannounced. I don't have a solution to this problem that doesn't involve violence.

However, the RVU concept allows you to define channels of communication which can be used for different purposes. You might train your family, friends and colleagues to send occasional urgent messages via SMS for example, a form of communication you've permitted to distract you. This way, you can tell them to expect slower responses to email which, being of higher volume and less urgency, you're checking less often. This will give you a much healthier relationship with your communications, allowing you to fix what could have been a psychotic relationship with your mail client and make smarter decisions about the kind of messages you send to others.

KEY POINTS

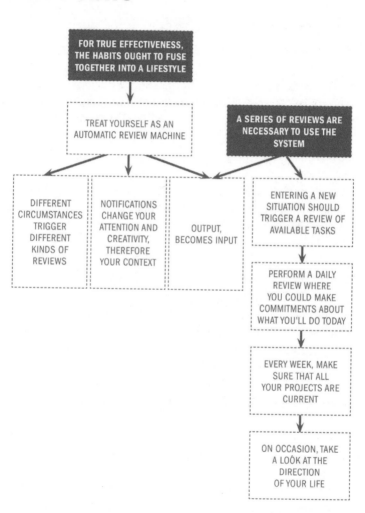

FOR TRUE EFFECTIVENESS, THE HABITS OUGHT TO FUSE TOGETHER INTO A LIFESTYLE

TREAT YOURSELF AS AN AUTOMATIC REVIEW MACHINE

A SERIES OF REVIEWS ARE NECESSARY TO USE THE SYSTEM

DIFFERENT CIRCUMSTANCES TRIGGER DIFFERENT KINDS OF REVIEWS

NOTIFICATIONS CHANGE YOUR ATTENTION AND CREATIVITY, THEREFORE YOUR CONTEXT

OUTPUT, BECOMES INPUT

ENTERING A NEW SITUATION SHOULD TRIGGER A REVIEW OF AVAILABLE TASKS

PERFORM A DAILY REVIEW WHERE YOU COULD MAKE COMMITMENTS ABOUT WHAT YOU'LL DO TODAY

EVERY WEEK, MAKE SURE THAT ALL YOUR PROJECTS ARE CURRENT

ON OCCASION, TAKE A LOOK AT THE DIRECTION OF YOUR LIFE

CONCLUSION

IMPLEMENTATION

I've tried to avoid dating this book by focusing on specific tools, especially digital tools. Instead, the assumption has been that, after a discussion of habits and theory (especially the entropy/abstraction concept), you'll be equipped to make informed decisions about the tools you'll use to implement these habits. I don't want the book to feel irrelevant in a few years' time because I wrote about the state-of-the-art as of 2015.

Your choice of tool is important for the reasons described in Habit 4: The Right Tools. If chosen well, a tool can enhance the quality of your work and the ease with which you can start working.

However, I think it's important to avoid getting too hung up on tool choice. I want to make a distinction between systems and processes.

A process is just a pattern of steps; that is, what the brain is doing while the hand is working. The way you manage tasks, paint pictures, write plays, or structure meetings are all examples of processes. A process can become a habit and it can last a lifetime.

Systems are the particular tools and technologies you use to implement your processes, such as your choice of computer, phone, stationery and so on. I cannot guarantee that I'll be using the same pair of trainers this time next month. It would be unwise for my running technique to become dependent upon a particular pair of shoes. It's also unlikely I'll be using the same computer for more than two or three years. This is just as well, since software and hardware evolve so fast. Don't build habits that depend upon such rapidly-shifting sands as a particular software programme. I want to focus on processes, which you can apply in whatever system suits you best. As technology changes you can choose new systems based on how well they reflect your processes.

Sometimes, technologies appear that enable new processes or create problems that give existing processes new meaning. Techniques for taking notes were enabled by the pen, and techniques for controlling an inbox didn't become urgent for most people until email and social media came along.

It's great when a technology gives birth to a new process, but let the process be weaned as soon as possible.

THE ADVANTAGE OF SOFTWARE

It's certainly possible to implement most of the most important habits, like *Habit 1: Capture*, using pen and paper, but I feel that these systems quickly become unwieldy if you need to modify the information they contain. This makes pen and paper unsuitable for the core of your task management system. Software does not suffer from this limitation.

FALLING OFF THE WAGON

I've not met anyone who sought to improve his or her productivity, who didn't encounter significant friction along the way, and give up. What should you do when this happens to you? I find (and your mileage may vary) that the process of falling-off-the-wagon and getting back on board is linked to the habit loop. It looked like this for me:

1. INTELLECTUAL INTEREST

When I first started to think about getting information out of my head, I found the idea very attractive. I hope after my presentation of it that you feel the same way. I was also impressed that I could solve what

I thought were inscrutable issues affecting my life. It's a particularly intense envy one feels when meeting a successful practitioner of some of these principles. I was quickly sold on the concept and I wanted to try it out.

2. RELIEF
This is quickly followed by a sense of relief at getting stuff off my mind into the safe environment of words and sentences. You might even enjoy it.

3. PANIC
The capture habit was followed by a mild sense of panic, especially at first. This is understandable, since I was producing a lot more information by getting it out of my head than I might have been holding in my head at one moment. I had a fairly extreme emotional reaction: "Look at all the undefined stuff I have left to do!"; "Where to begin?"; "This looks impossible!"; "I will never change."

4. RESOLUTION
Working down the list of tasks as described in Habit 2: Processing eases that sense of panic. Take the list and work top down, each task in turn. Don't even look at the other tasks. You will begin to gain a sense of control and relaxation at this point. But it won't yet be a habit; something which happens automatically without thinking about it. For now, these activities will need prompting and reminders.

5. FRICTION
Most of the habits in this book are simple, common sense stuff; most of which you're probably already doing in one form or another. But asking you to do them in a consistent, watertight way is probably asking you to break the habit of a lifetime. It's easy to let stuff accumulate in the mind, and while few people could deny that this is destructive, in the moment it's easier to do nothing. For those who

do take notes, the problem is often one of consistency. Should you write down every idea, note or commitment into a single place? Do you regularly process that information? Before these habits become internalized and automatic it's inevitable that you'll hit a wall.

When the habit is triggered, prepare to invest a little bit of effort and endure a little bit of friction. The work is front-loaded, meaning you have to do it right now. The investment pays off later on, but in the moment it can feel like a significant cost, not an investment. And so you give up. Before long, a mess accumulates. Notes lie everywhere, commitments are not written down, the calendar does not reflect reality, and you forget your own ideas. It's at this point that your inner critic says "I told you so; nothing will change." And so you fall off the wagon. Actually, this is a good thing. It gives you a perfect opportunity to compare the old way of doing things to what you've experienced of the new. When you decide to get back on the wagon, the process is easier.

6. BACK ON THE WAGON

- Take your capture system and write down everything that's accumulated in your mind.
- You'll probably have lots of "oh yeah" moments.
- Record any pressing, incomplete tasks that have been bothering you.
- Turn your unread emails, messages and notes into properly-written tasks.
- Once you've processed the stuff you've captured, focus on the positive feelings of control and completion that you will experience.

The brain dump exercise gives you a safety net which will catch you while you're developing the habit. You will probably encounter more friction which will knock you off the wagon again. That's absolutely fine - it will happen many times. Pick yourself back up again.

7. HABIT FORMS

Over time, the habit will form. You will begin to internalize the process; your brain associating the routine with the trigger. When this happens, you'll need to think less and less about performing the habit, and will find that it becomes automatic. When this happens, the mess that you create can become a good thing. As you'll see later, mess is what happens when you create cool stuff. Knowing how to get yourself back on the wagon allows you to tidy it up, creating space for you to make a mess.

THE INNER CRITIC

Your inner critic is an enemy to your ability to adopt new habits. Its chief tactic is to convince you that change is impossible. It works by remaining mute, gathering information and forming patterns; noticing that work is front-loaded and requiring effort at first. These patterns will inform your doubts. It's best to force the inner critic to speak up for itself when you're struggling to adopt a habit. Use the capture habit to write out any negative thoughts associated with your work and the process. This act will cause you to become self-aware for a moment, forcing the inner critic to disgorge its voice, and so letting you refute it with rationality and reason.

FINAL THOUGHTS

These habits should become a lifestyle; something you do without question or effort. Like brushing your teeth or making your bed, it's just something you do.

I hope that the habits in this book are comfortable for you now, and that you've gained mastery and perspective. The habits in this book, when implemented, will help you to regain the reins that control the information in your life. You'll make better decisions and do work which befits the capabilities of your mind. You should now have insight into the principles and processes that support productive behaviour.

Moreover, perhaps it has helped you to think systemically about the way in which you work with information, especially the cycles of capture and review, and the triggers which begin these cycles. These processes form a kind of externalized cognition, where large parts of your thinking processes occur outside your head, using physical systems. It's important that the processes, which these habits support, become watertight in order that you develop the trust necessary to rely on those systems and ultimately, get into the habit of finishing what you start. When this occurs, you'll have created a kind of second external brain which augments innate weaknesses in the way you deal with information, so allowing the mind to work to its natural strengths.

What's most important is that I hope that the book has given you confidence that things can change. Return to the book in a few months, once you've started using the habits it describes. Let it be not just a guide but a reference too, particularly if you need reminding about what you gain from each habit. For more, including articles, papers and a comprehensive list of the tools I use personally, visit my site: www.inkandben.com/tph

CONSOLIDATING THE HABITS

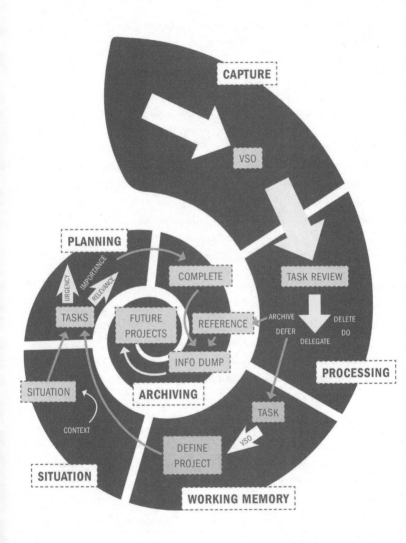

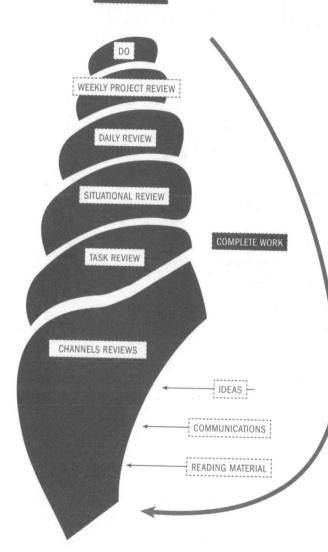

VOLUME OF INFO

RELEVANCE

DO

WEEKLY PROJECT REVIEW

DAILY REVIEW

SITUATIONAL REVIEW

COMPLETE WORK

TASK REVIEW

CHANNELS REVIEWS

IDEAS

COMMUNICATIONS

READING MATERIAL

ABOUT THE AUTHOR

ABOUT BEN ELIJAH

Ben Elijah is a coach, speaker, and author. He developed his early career in some of the world's biggest technology firms. After overcoming the issues described in his book, he began working with individuals and organizations, helping them build a better relationship with conflicting information in a complex world.

Contact the author for advice, coaching, mentoring and speaking

Website for the book: www.inkandben.com/tph
 @inkandben